#BYOP

PRAISE FOR *#BYOP: BE YOUR OWN PRODUCER*

"*#BYOP* is a must-read for any artist who is ready to achieve their highest potential! If you're done waiting for someone else to hand you your dreams and are ready to get in the driver's seat and create them yourself, this book will be your coach and inspiration for every step of the way."

Ali Stroker,
Tony Award-winning actress for *Oklahoma!*

"I've always found Ashley Kate to be one of the most courageous and innovative people, so it's no surprise to me at all that she wrote this book. If you've ever wanted to create your own work and feel unsure where to start or need to feel inspired to do so, this book is for you."

Jonathan Demar,
Tony Award-winning producer of *Hadestown*

"Ashley Kate Adams is the definition of #girlboss! Her knowledge, positive outlook, and stories throughout this book keep you glued from page one. Heck, I'd pay a million dollars for some Ashley Kate Adams advice, and lucky for you, it's just the price of one book."

Sainty Nelsen,
three-time Emmy Award-winning producer;
Tony Award nominated producer; actress in
Sex & Drugs & Rock & Roll and *Trolls: The Beat Goes On!*

"This book is a PERFECT companion to anyone who wants to create their own work. Ashley Kate is able to expertly explain the process of creation and gives you all the tools you need to get started. As a producer myself, I plan on reading this book repeatedly."

Sarah Seeds,
actress; producer; SAG-AFTRA board member
(National and New York)

"I LOVED reading this book so much! *#BYOP* hits home on the importance of trusting and pushing yourself, and gives a play-by-play on how to manage your own mind and expectations while still finding JOY in your life and work."

Lauren "LOLO" Pritchard,
songwriter for Panic! At the Disco (double platinum
for *Death of a Bachelor,* 2020 BMI Pop Awards nominee
for *High Hopes*); solo music artist

"*#BYOP* is the definitive self-help book for creatives who need a little push to be their own producer and create art on their own terms. Reading this book is like having a business heart-to-heart conversation with your best friend: someone who believes in you, and wants to empower you!"

Remy Zaken,
actress in the original Broadway company of *Spring Awakening*

"Ashley Kate has managed to create a hybrid self-help book/exorcism manual. Through anecdotes and instructions, she has laid down how she navigated the journey to becoming a producer. In the "worts and all" pages of this book, you may very well find the seeds you need to plant your own producer's garden."

David Errigo Jr.,
voiceover actor for *Phineas and Ferb: The Movie* and *Pokémon*

"Ashley Kate's daring vulnerability about her own producing journey provides invaluable insight into what it truly means to create from the heart of your own unique experiences. In an industry that seems impossibly out of control, *#BYOP* helps you discover your creative footing, and encourages you to bravely take the reins of your own journey."

Kelly Lamor Wilson,
actress of *Freaky* and *Summer '03*

"*#BYOP* is a must have in your multi-hyphenate creative tool belt. Ashley Kate writes with extreme care and vivid imagery that can guide any creator as they head out on their own journey. *#BYOP's* ideas and achievable challenges are applicable for today, tomorrow, and the future. Not only will you be a better artist, you'll be a better human being."

Michael Kushner,
Dear Multi-Hyphenate podcast

#BYOP

BE YOUR OWN PRODUCER

ASHLEY KATE ADAMS

NEW YORK

LONDON • NASHVILLE • MELBOURNE • VANCOUVER

#BYOP

Be Your Own Producer

Published in New York, New York, by Morgan James Publishing. Morgan James is a trademark of Morgan James, LLC. www.MorganJamesPublishing.com

ISBN 9781631953644 paperback
ISBN 9781631953651 eBook
ISBN 9781631953668 audiobook
Library of Congress Control Number: 2020947979

Cover Design by:
Patryk Larney

Interior Design by:
Christopher Kirk
www.GFSstudio.com

Morgan James is a proud partner of Habitat for Humanity Peninsula and Greater Williamsburg. Partners in building since 2006.

Get involved today! Visit
MorganJamesPublishing.com/giving-back

For my parents.
To my daddy, Ernie Adams. Thank you for being my creative
sounding board while you were here on this earth, and for always
encouraging me to think bigger than myself. Thank you for
guiding me with your energy as I continue on my creative journey
now. To my mom, Dana Jo Adams. Thank you for being a strong
example of order and limitless ideas. Thank you for showing me
how to be brave and consistent. Your resilience inspires me every
day. Thank you for nurturing my creative spirit.

TABLE OF CONTENTS

ACKNOWLEDGMENT

Before we get started, I want to acknowledge **YOU**. Yes, YOU! Whether you're just rolling out of bed, or snuggled into a Manhattan coffee shop ready with your notebook in hopes of learning something new... *Thank you* for joining me on this journey today as we talk about our creativity.

I want to acknowledge you first, because without you, this wouldn't be a conversation. Without you taking action to open this book, it would probably just sit on a shelf, useless and collecting dust. Thank you for encouraging my creativity by taking a chance on this millennial from Kentucky who now calls New York City her creative home. Thank you for jumping in with me. Thank you for sharing your energy with me, and above all, thank you for sharing your time, focus, and dreams with me.

Today I want to give you the keys to my castle. By joining me, you'll be hearing a little bit about my creative journey, and I hope that my vulnerability with you about my heart, path, and creativity, encourages *your* journey. Seriously, nothing gives me greater happiness.

If you felt called to grab this book, you might be at a roadblock within your creative identity, or stuck between ideas. Maybe you're feeling frozen at the moment, or in the middle of your own personal creative reinvention. You might even be in the middle of rising back up after a project landed in a completely different place than you thought it would. Or you may have just been screwed over for the first time (or the tenth) after being really brave and you feel like your intentions and ideas aren't being heard.

I want you to know that this is a safe place. While I do believe these conversations are extra magical and can inspire limitless expression, I am coming to you from inside a book. There is some space in between. Everything you create is sacred—it is yours, and it belongs to you. Relish this time to create in the here and now, and I'll be here on the side to encourage you. Throughout this book, I'm also going to share with you some ways to keep your creativity and heart protected.

I hope you don't finish this book. Okay, that sounded bad. I hope you *do* finish this book at some point, but I hope you don't finish it in one sitting. My wish for you is to have some things unlocked inside of you during this little conversation we're having. I want you to *want* to put this book down and start something new. I want you to throw it across the room and run to your computer or notepad, ready to rock on your latest and greatest idea. Or if you feel like chucking it, you can do that too.

The exciting news is that what you're destined to be is already inside you. You already hold all of the keys to your castle. I am not a guru, and I won't claim to know anything about your specific journey. I can only share a bit of my journey with you in hopes to reveal that the only thing you're probably missing is action. Today, above all things, I am here to encourage you to create.

So, let's get to it! I know I have you for a very limited time, and I know you'll be throwing this book aside at some point in the very near future.

Oh, and one last thing... **I believe in YOU!**

INTRODUCTION

I t was truly the best of times. I was 23, fresh out of college from what is considered one of the top musical theatre schools in the nation, and making my Broadway debut joining the cast of the Tony Award-winning revival of *La Cage Aux Folles* written by the great Harvey Fierstein, and composed by the beloved, late Jerry Herman. This revival, hailing from London and directed by Terry Johnson, was a dream come true. Not to mention it was the talk of the town for its presentation, incredible ensemble of nightclub dancers and drag queens (known as the Cagelles), and tender subject matter.

If you aren't familiar, *La Cage* is a musical about two older gay men proudly running a nightclub in St. Tropez in the face of all adversity—even the kind found within their own household when their straight son brings home his fiancé, Anne, and her incredibly conservative parents.

After leaning heavily on my personality to get me through a ballet dance call, I had hit the working actress jackpot. I was going to make my Broadway debut with a speaking role in a well-respected show—one that directed me to eat Nutella while walking sassily across the stage in 4-inch wedges and a crop top! It. Was. *Everything.* I knew in that moment, as my heart pounded out of my chest while I waited in the wings of the Longacre Theatre, that I was lucky to be where I was. This magical moment in time would never happen again. You only debut once.

When I arrived at the theatre for my first performance, it looked like a florist's dream. Flowers and plants were everywhere as I entered through the backstage door; I felt like Audrey in *Little Shop of Horrors*. The gentleman at the stage door handed me a telegram from my parents in Kentucky upon my arrival, and Harvey Fierstein welcomed me kindly into his dressing room on my way up to the fourth floor. Harvey was also currently starring in the show in the role of Albin, opposite the incredible Christopher Sieber. As I said before, it was truly the best of times.

Opening Night went off without a hitch! The cast was loving and supportive, and I got to celebrate with my new Broadway family next door at our old saloon haunt, Hurley's. I joined the company after just two weeks of one-on-one rehearsal with our lovely dance captain, Christophe, and resident director, Tony. Try learning a big musical without any other actors or dancers around you... it's quite the experience. But everything I had worked for was officially paying off.

The next morning, I woke up bursting with sunshine. It was my first double show day on *Broadway!* I was looking forward to spending more time with my new castmates in between shows, and hearing more about the secret Sardi's menu after our matinee.

We kicked off the show like normal. Half-dressed, I went down behind the curtain to sing back-up for our Cagelles onstage, and watched as they performed one of the most extraordinary opening numbers I had ever seen. They did this eight-times a week; complete with tap dancing, costume changes, jump-splits, and more. Everyone singing back-up on the opening number would make faces at each other backstage while watching the performers onstage. I couldn't believe this was my JOB.

During intermission of the matinee show, as I was changing into my blue poncho for the start of Act Two, I got a text from my mom saying that she and my dad had just landed, and were in a cab on their way to the theater. I sent her instructions about what to say when they got to the stage door, and our stage manager's voice came over the speaker, "First half is going great! Can we please get everyone in the house after the show for a full company meeting?"

I looked at my dressing roommates for guidance, and Cheryl, one of the sweetest and most talented character actresses in the biz, looked back at me and said with her big eyes, *oh no.*

"Well, maybe you'll get to play Anne on tour," said another castmate.

I giggled it off. *What? Going on tour? I just got here!* I had *just* started this job yesterday! It hadn't even been 24-hours since I walked into the theatre with purpose and job security, and my fancy six-month contract in my proverbial pocket. I barely remember my scene partners' real names at this point.

Slowly, the rest of the show started to feel a little more somber. I noticed the cast getting more emotional than normal during our full company number, *The Best of Times*. I looked around at everyone onstage, tapping their prop champagne flutes together with eye contact that's half full of joy, and half terror. There was a weird energy on stage, like everyone was really embracing the lyrics. *So, make this moment last, because the best of times is now.*

The curtain came down, and I hung up my blue poncho and made my way into the house of the Longacre Theatre. *We're almost there!* My mom's text read. I used this as an opportunity to quickly thank the producers in person for the job before taking a seat with the rest of the cast, who waited with tight smiles on their face.

Finally, our producer, Barry Weissler, stood up next to his wife and gave a beautiful speech about the year-and-a-half journey of our incredible show. He moved us as he reminisced about the rehearsal process and opening night, and celebrated being nominated for the Tony's and *winning* said Tony's. He talked about how we're all family at this point, and I felt so blessed. I couldn't believe that I got to be a part of telling this incredible story.

Mr. Weissler concluded his warm speech, took a deep breath, and clasped his hands together...

"I'm sorry to say that our beautiful show will be closing at the end of the month."

• • •

Suddenly the sands of St. Tropez had turned into quicksand. My life, my joy, my certainty and security, and my dream just *froze* out in the balance in front of me. I was in shock. Everything I had worked and hoped for just crumbled in an instant before my eyes. And because I was still on such a high from my Broadway debut the night before, I could barely process what was happening. Thank God my parents were right outside.

To see their happy faces as they hugged and congratulated me on my big Broadway opening, only to tell them we had just gotten the closing notice on the rebound of the embrace completely broke my heart.

We all skipped Sardi's, and my parents and I parted so I could get to the theater for call time of the evening show. After climbing the four flights to my dressing room, I just stood there, staring at my costumes. There was a shift of energy inside of me. As Cheryl's eyes had said before, *oh, no*.

At this point in my life, I had never grieved anything before. I'd never been one to rest on my laurels or expect anything, but this just didn't make sense. At all. But most of all, what didn't make sense to me was the shift happening inside me.

That is until now.

This experience was the beginning of my bountiful and unexpected path as a creative in New York City.

It was time to be brave. Even braver than before. It was time to figure out my own path, and create the ability to do so again and again. It was time for me to be my own producer.

#BYOP

PART ONE
IDENTITY

1

NO ONE CAN GIVE YOU PERMISSION TO CREATE BUT YOURSELF

There, I said it. *No one can give you permission to create but yourself.* No director holds the keys, no studio, no casting director, no gallery owner... it is you, and you alone, baby!

At the start of my career I was hungry for people to ask me to do things. I wanted people to invite me places; to always be included, both personally and creatively. I wanted to be asked to audition for the most exciting projects, and to be invited to sing somewhere. I wanted to be thought of by others. But the truth is, I wanted to be thought of by others *to fuel my creativity*.

Not that wanting that was wrong, as to me there is no wrong when it comes to art. But from a very young age, it was more about what others wanted me to do, and what they wanted to hear from me.

Maybe it's because I was raised in Kentucky into a Broadway loving family and a community that cultivated strong musical theatre performers... or maybe it was because at the time, I never really understood what a producer was. For me, being talented meant that I was a strong Broadway style musical theater performer.

That was my identity.

And it carried me far. I got into the best school in the nation for performing arts, and was on that Broadway stage exactly two years after my U-Haul pulled into Washington Heights, Manhattan in 2009.

Then came the reality.

As a performer, what you mainly do is audition. I know that might seem strange, but the truth is, when you're a professional with a hungry and hardworking agent, you are always auditioning. They submit you for a role based on someone else's description of their project, and you get invited to audition based on your headshot and resume, or what they think you can do.

I found myself more fascinated than frustrated with this concept, but I had to have a very honest moment of truth with myself: my life and how I was spending my time was solely based on what others wanted for me. I spent my time as people told me to (or how they had allowed me to spend it). And if someone didn't give me the green light, I wasn't able to do what I'm most passionate about. This realization shocked me to my core.

It took $80,000 of debt from musical theatre school to recognize this was the reality. Not to mention the upset of my big Broadway debut closing so soon. I had to find a way to do what I loved all the time, regardless of being invited or not.

I meditated on it. I cried about it. I felt depressed about it. I felt like I was journeying through a crowded forest, battling my way through vines and fallen trees, trying to find my way out. I was trying to find my true, authentic voice as an artist. Once I finally allowed myself to take that journey of curiosity, the clarity came. I will never forget this moment—I was walking toward the water in Long Island City (my new neighborhood), and suddenly it was so incredibly clear to me: *no one can give you permission to create but yourself.*

I froze, but this time in a positive way. The clouds opened, and I felt joy for the first time in a very long time. *This is my life and I can choose to express myself any way I want. I have been the one keeping myself in chains and forcing myself on a much smaller path than the one my heart truly desires.*

I had been so caught up in what others were asking me to do that I had completely overlooked the bottom line: at my core, I was an *artist*. An artist with an active choice, and stories to tell. I had a desire in me to get messy, and to create and express myself in a much deeper way than I was letting myself do. I was struggling with my identity, and as an artist I hadn't arrived yet because I didn't know who I was. But for the first time in a long time, I once again yearned to create. I finally gave myself permission.

So, what kind of permission do you need to give yourself today? Is it permission to create? To claim your true identity or explore new parts of your expression? Do you need to give yourself permission to take a break, or get a little louder? Do you need to ask someone to support your creative ideas, or to be your teammate? Have you been wanting to try something new? Finally, are you currently a reflection of your most authentic self?

If you feel yourself starting to breathe a little deeper, or your soul is starting to rise up out of your chest with something more to say... I know in my heart we might be onto something—starting today.

THE FEAR OF FAILURE, PART 1

Fear always comes two-fold. Part one is the fear of failing to achieve your current goals and dreams. In the creative and performing arts world, sometimes we feel there's an imaginary window of time with an expiration date that we either create for ourselves, or we feel the industry has created for us—a window of limited time to be discovered or to book Broadway. If we don't achieve our goal within that time, we're a failure. When we feel like a failure, the depression train hits, the wind gets knocked out of our creative sails, and like a pool float in early September, we begin to deflate.

You want to hear something funny? When I was a tween, I had an internal goal to be on Broadway by the age of sixteen. *SIXTEEN!* Bless my inner child, she was just as ambitious as her grown-up version today, but that crazy expectation fueled a lot for me. I would privately check in about this and hold myself accountable. I was lucky that when that didn't happen, I kept trudging on, setting new goals and benchmarks to keep moving forward. But there was still that little voice inside that would sometimes whisper in my ear, *welp, you didn't make it in time.* Funny, right? It's especially funny when you hear this from a child's perspective, but how many times do we say this to ourselves as adult creatives every day?

We do this a lot. We say to ourselves there is only one way to achieve our lifelong goals and dreams. We make this invisible electric fence from the judgement of others, or our judgement of them. We qualify other people's career jumps or life moves, and immediately compare and take it inward, making it about us. We say to ourselves that there is only one timeline in which we will proudly function. My question to you is, *why do we keep limiting ourselves?* Let's sucker punch fear in the face, my fellow creatives! Fear is an emotion that you are fully capable of standing up to. Don't let it bully you. There is truly no such thing as failure, there is only moving forward.

STAY IN YOUR LANE

But what about Sheila, who just graduated from the college that I didn't get into? She just walked right into her first audition room and booked a Broadway show! Well first of all, I'm writing to you from inside a pandemic—is that Broadway show even open?

Do you see what I mean? These constraints, this electric fence we've created for ourselves, doesn't really exist. And when we stay in our lane, we can use that energy more productively and focus on something that we actually have control over: ourselves, and our own creativity.

I know it's challenging to stay in our own lane, but comparison truly is the thief of joy. You don't have to waste time spiraling down rabbit holes on social media, you can choose to put the phone down. You don't have to sit at parties (or on Zoom calls) and waste your time picking apart and comparing others' success or their ability to move forward. If you struggle with letting others be or with celebrating where they are, then you're most likely struggling to let yourself just be who you are, and celebrating that. So, let's live and create the way we want to and encourage others to do the same. That seems fair to me, and I promise it's a much easier way to live inside what can sometimes be an exhausting career path.

When we stay in our lane, it helps us to realize that all we need to do is keep chugging along in our own way, down our own individual path. Can you see how much joy and creative freedom there is in this?

IF WE FEAR LETTING DOWN OTHERS, WE MAY IN TURN LET DOWN OURSELVES

If we fear letting others down by creating in a different way than what they had originally expected from us, or let that noise pivot our original game plan or what we want, we might start living and creating for other people, and not ourselves. This should be our greatest fear: that we are not living and creating authentically.

It's a tragedy if we go through life every day with a story inside us, but never find the courage to share it. If you would rather tell your own story than share someone else's, that is okay. If you're like me and want to be a "non-discriminant" storyteller, that's okay too. I personally identify with being a storyteller first, and when I'm drawn to a story, I want to help tell it in whatever way I can, no matter what the medium, or what my role is in telling it. (More on this later!) Creativity is not brain surgery, but if we limit ourselves, it has the ability to break our hearts.

Give yourself permission to allow yourself to create for *you*, too. You see how this quickly comes back to the main topic from this chapter, *no one can give you permission to create but yourself.* So, let's start to explore that new found permission together, now that we're claiming it! Let's continue to walk on through. I've got you. We've only got one shot at living, so we have a responsibility as artists to share the stories that only we can tell.

THE FEAR OF FAILURE, PART 2

When I first began encouraging and coaching other artists to navigate all of the many corners of their creativity, the number one thing that I wanted was to debunk the fear of starting something new. Fear itself seems to be such an intangible thing—a massive emotion and familiar response that has the ability to freeze us wherever we are, and control our behavior, actions, and choices. As artists, we know that it sometimes has the ability to keep us somewhere we don't want to be for too long, in fear of losing an opportunity or a working relationship. But sometimes we simply have the fear of starting something new.

Yes, simply. By simple, I mean that this kind of fear is often a restraint we place on ourselves, and not actually the reality of what will happen when we start something new. As artists, sometimes we project our thoughts onto an opportunity, idea, or a collaboration because our imagination begins to run wild, and the fear starts to take over.

One of my #BYOP Challenges to you is to *remain open past fear.* What if this new idea, opportunity, collaboration, or expression you're afraid of unlocks both you and your future? What if that thing you are currently afraid of could become your happy place? That sounds pretty important, right? Shouldn't this be something that you should at least *explore*? I think yes! 500 percent, YES!

Throughout this book we will explore these new lanes together. We'll explore the twists and turns of creating your own content, creating and collaborating with others, and most importantly how to *be your own producer.* How to be your own producer of both content and creative freedom. How to be your own producer of happiness, and how to be your own producer of your future, again and again.

2

YOU'RE AN ARTIST FIRST

I don't know why, but when I hear the word *artist*, I first envision a painter holding up a paint brush, brow furled, working on his painting overlooking the Seine in Paris. To me, for some reason, I defined the word artist as the creator of visual arts, and because of that, I was *not* an artist. I always identified with being a *performer* and not a performing *artist* (even though it's literally what my high school was called).

What about you? When you hear the word artist, what do you immediately think of? What is the first image that comes to your mind? When I say ballet dancer or Tik-Tok star, do you first think of them as artists? It feels a little weird, right? What about when I say sculptor, painter, or craftsmen? You're probably thinking, *now that's an artist.*

In ways, we've trained ourselves as a society to put some performers on a pedestal, and others not—giving some the power to cross over into celebrity or influencer status. What I'm more concerned about is how this pertains to *us:* the people in the middle who aren't publicly regarded as either celebrities, influencers, or high-end artists, but instead are working performers and visual artists who juggle survival jobs to make their dreams come true.

A decade ago, in the first few months of the early parts of my career, I had the opportunity to star in the title role of an original musical in New York City, *The Gay Bride of Frankenstein.* It was a really cool experience. I was painted with a full face of makeup every show like a blue Elphaba, and I got to sing with my own personal rock band. I was living dreams. Both the show and the role were monumental for me. Not only was it the first role that people began to identify me with (we talked about that need earlier), it was an extremely collaborative and creative process. And because of that collaborative process, it allowed me my first opportunity to help produce a property.

One summer day, I was hanging out with the writer and composer of *Gay Bride*, Billy Butler (one of the most gifted artists I know), and his loving wife Paula, talking about my desire to get more involved in the future development of the show. I was interested in hearing more about his new musical ideas for the show, and I wanted to share my ideas to help take it to the next step. I also wanted to know more about all of the moving pieces that made up this production. I remember asking if I was a 'weird' actress for wanting to know more about all of these things.

Billy looked at me and said, "You're not weird, you're an artist."

An artist?! Wow, am I fancy! An *artist*! This is when the clouds first started cracking open for me. I thought, *if I'm an artist, this means that I, too, can roll around in my artistry*. And this must mean I can roll around in different forms of artistic expressions, too. Don't ask me why at this point I didn't think being an artist pertained to me. Maybe it had to do with breaking the rules? Yes, that was definitely it.

Billy will always have one of the greatest influences on my journey. He was one of the first people that I collaborated with who did more than one thing as an artist. He was an amazing example. Collaborating with him gave me additional permission. I was encouraged and welcomed to think the way I did, and he reassured me that by thinking that way, it would only help make the show better. I'm proud to say that it very much *did* help to nurture the next decade of the show. I took what little money I'd saved from my month-and-a-half on Broadway, and I became a second producer for the show. Since the music was one of the show's stars, I felt we should do a showcase presentation with its current singers, one of them being myself. It was the very first evidence of me being my own producer.

When I first told my mom that I might venture into writing this book, I asked her if she thought it was too big of an idea. I asked once again, "Is that weird?" Is it weird for a young woman who had mainly expressed herself as an actor, singer, and producer to now write a book?

"For you, it's not."

I decided to take that as a compliment.

What this all boils down to is artistic freedom and our true identities. If we are artists, it's not weird if one day we want to paint, and the next day we want to sing. It's not weird that one day we might begin to dance while running lines in our head, and then immediately feel the need to sign up for a dance class despite having two left feet. It's not weird that while reading this you might think, *if she can do it, maybe I can step forward with that book idea too*. This is the name of the game. If we enjoy dabbling in different forms of art, could you imagine the joy we might feel if we allow ourselves to embrace *all* of the forms of artistic expression? It's like an unending treasure chest of exploration, challenges, and happiness.

TRIPPED UP IN PERFECTIONISM

I am a perfectionist, tried and true. The craziest thing is, with being a perfectionist you're usually aware of every aspect of your personality because awareness is part of your survival process. You watch every move you make so that you can criticize it, revamp it, and hold yourself to outlandish expectations, forcing yourself to be the best version of you (or so you think). I knew I was very particular about some things in my life, but I had no idea that I was a perfectionist.

My earliest clue of perfectionism was in an improv class at one of those model scouting agencies in Kentucky. I was sitting in the front seat of an imaginary car playing the alphabet road trip game with another student, and every sentence we said had to start with the next letter of the alphabet. All I kept thinking was, *can I please pull this car over and get out? This is the worst thing I have ever made myself do to better my acting career.*

I was terrified of improv. Terrified! And to this day, I think that personal terror helps me when I teach it to other children. When I teach, I look at these kids and talk to them like I would my own inner child. *Try not to judge yourself. Try to just allow yourself to be present in the moment and respond. Don't worry what others might think about what comes out of your mouth, they're only worried about what they're going to say.* And it's all true! But this need for perfectionism—to do everything right and not mess up—tripped me up so much as a child and still perches up on my shoulder at times even as an adult.

We want to be right. We want people's approval. We want people to appreciate our hard work. But I want to encourage you to not get tripped up in your own perfectionism. When we begin to expand or try new things, it's going to get messy. That's one of my favorite things I have learned from working with kids: they don't care if they get messy! They throw themselves into every-thing, especially their new creative ideas and explorations. I wish this same kind of peace, joy, and creative freedom for us. It's time to get out the finger paints! Maybe then we'll rock on over to an improv class.

VALUE YOUR MAGIC

So, what does it mean for you to value your magic as an artist? I feel like we hear this phrase all the time. In order to value ourselves as *artists*, we need to acknowledge and value *ourselves* firsts. Output-ting art into the world can create magic. As I mentioned in Chapter 1, sometimes as artists we feel the need to seek others' approval. That approval must begin with us. The way we actively treat our-selves is what alerts the Universe (and others) on how to treat and/ or value us. And yes, this largely includes working relationships.

Spending my twenties in NYC, I learned many lessons about valuing my magic the hard way. This is one of the many reasons I felt called to write this book. I got burned a lot, which we will dis-cuss later on. My personal and creative disconnect was that I wasn't valuing my magic. I was jumping into projects too fast, and was so eager to form new creative business relationships that at times I was doing so blindly. If we value our magic, we understand it's okay to take our time, especially when starting a new thing. It's okay to need a moment to process, observe, and reset before we take action.

You, my dear and boundless creative, hold magic. You hold every key you will ever need inside of you. Let us celebrate this value together through your new ideas and work as we navigate the challenges ahead.

CREATING YOUR ART-MOSPHERE

One of the ways we value our magic is through the 'art-mosphere' we create to execute our work in. All of these things matter because they affect the vibrations of your working space and therefore affect the energy you provide for others.

When I step into teaching a new class, setting a new show, or producing a new project at AKA Studio Productions, we practice *ego out the door* to help to create a productive art-mosphere. It's a simple way of encouraging your new creative collaborators and shows that you welcome them to feel comfortable in their new found working space. By using this practice, all will be heard. Ego got us into the room and now we have to push it outside of the room in order to safely collaborate and create as a team. When we put our egos aside, it allows us to better create a safe space for all.

Have you ever been in a rehearsal process, writer's room, or songwriting session with a person who feels really closed off or abruptly abrasive? It makes you feel uncomfortable, right? This is usually the type of creative who might have random outbursts or say something that makes you feel less vulnerable in your safe creative space.

All that person is trying to do is assert themselves. We want to acknowledge this, and the best way to do so is through warmth and connection. If we're focused on creating a positive art-mosphere for (and with) them, a simple thing we can do is reach out a hand, or ask them how they're doing and what they need.

Creating that productive art-mosphere starts at the top, so if you find yourself in the driver's seat and leading a show or a class, producing your own work, or owning a small creative business, *you* should lead the environment. As you continue to expand your creative endeavors, you'll come in contact with more creatives of all personality types. Make sure you're doing your best to show ego the door and trust that by practicing this, incredible results will follow.

YOUR ARTIST'S RECIPE

You are an artist, and with your artistry comes your very own special recipe! There is no right or wrong way to create, but there is your very own way—a way in which you are the most comfortable, happy, and connected, and therefore the most productive.

Do you create best in the mornings or at night? Do you need people around you to feel motivated? Do you need to keep people away so that you can focus? What about a combination of the two? Do you have the budget to have an office or would you rather spend that money somewhere else? Do you know in your heart that you have to save up to buy that studio space, so you need to round up friends to split it with you in the meantime? There is no right or wrong answer, but there are YOUR answers. You need to do this kind of investigative work for yourself so you can create most efficiently. As you grow, and if/when you have to work with others, you need to know how to describe what you need for how you can be the most productive. The answer to these questions is your very own artist's recipe!

Personally, I've got to be in my own little quiet space to do my best work. Knowing this, I built my production company right at home on my own kitchen table. It's easy, and I know I'll be comfortable. I don't have to travel or commute, and my coffee maker and fridge are only six-feet away. At the end of each day, I stack everything back to the office side of the table. Voila! I have my own personal home office with zero additional overhead cost. Insert wink face here.

ROME WASN'T BUILT IN A DAY

I mentioned earlier that I am a perfectionist. Is there anyone else here peeking through these pages who might feel similarly? Hello, my people! Perfectionists like things to move fast and efficiently, but this work—the largest being ourselves—can take some time. So, claim that newfound artistry proudly! Also remember that when exploring new and unknown territory, you'll need to take *time* to discover and play to prepare for creating your own way.

3

CREATE YOUR OWN WAY

O nce we acknowledge that we hold the keys to our own creative freedom, that's when the true party begins. It's like that scene from *The Wizard of Oz,* where Dorothy steps out of her midwestern, black-and-white world, right onto the bedazzled yellow brick road, led by curiosity, and bathed in technicolor. When you connect with all of the *true* parts of yourself (including your creativity), you just breathe differently. Suddenly your daily routine has morphed into a pool of endless possibility, and you want to jump right in and swim with all of the ideas that you're finally letting yourself feel. You're ready to make a big splash! For me it felt like a celebration. As we ask every time we meet on #BYOP Live: "How are you feeling today?"

Are you feeling the creative fuzzies? Is your mind starting to race in a bazillion different directions? Enjoy it! Relish in it! Call your mom! Write it down so you don't forget. Run out in the street if you want! Tell the man who made your sandwich today at the deli that you're having a great day because you're ready to claim all of the creativity and possibilities in your life.

You have always had the ability to create your own way, you just needed a little nudge first to continue moving forward in that direction. Are you ready? This will be one of the hardest things you'll ever do, but I promise it will also be the most freeing.

ADDING A PATH

My favorite part about creating our own way is that within this new possibility, we still get to claim all of our previous magic, our history, and where we came from. We still get to claim our artistic or business journey that led us to this point. These journeys are incredibly important because the paths that we've already taken are what will inform our creativity and curiosity leading us into our future. And have no fear, just because we're starting to feel different tingling sensations about our new sense of creativity doesn't mean we have to ditch our other forms of creativity—though you can if you feel called to.

But in case no one told you today... you are allowed to have it all. *You can do both*. I'm going to say it again for the people in the back, YOU CAN DO BOTH! You can have it all *if* you are ready to claim it. You can create in all of the ways at the same time! You can do it all, and together we'll start to explore how to navigate all of the opportunities this will create for both you and your future.

FUEL THE FIRE

You are allowed to have it all. I don't understand the people who like to tell us no or that we can't. Better yet, I don't understand the people who give you their advice while they're stuck in a job or life choice that doesn't make them happy, making them project all of their own irrational fears onto you. These people somehow make the conversation about *your* own creative journey and identity.

For you my darling reader, I had to include this: remember that others should stay in their own lane. That person, colleague, parent who didn't go after their dream, or lover (who you now might want to get rid of) can share their own judgements of you, but they are not your truth. Only *you* know that. And because of these naysayers with less hopeful visions, we must learn to nurture our spirits so we can continue to grow *around* them.

Let these people be the fuel to your fire. I'll be extremely honest with you: I love that it shocks people that as a young woman, I'm also a producer. I'll credit that to the song *Broadway Baby,* in the bridge that goes, "Hey, Mr. Producer ..." I personally find so much joy in being a producer and *not* being a mister. I love that it's unexpected. I love that it's unassuming because it lets me do so much more creative work and sly observation. Do you know how many times people have looked at me sideways because I was claiming my true identity?

I remember earlier on, when I was first starting to blossom in my additional creative path, I was speaking on a panel for a non-profit theatre company in the heart of midtown. The panel included three men over 40... and me. As I spoke about how I ran my business, they looked dumbfounded. They couldn't believe I worked out of my kitchen, as they complained about their overhead costs for their fancy offices. I kindly celebrated that by working from home, I could put any extra funds I have back into my projects. As they were complaining about these costs (with not many current properties to show for it), I thought, *well your problems and solutions seem extremely clear to me*. Looking back, I now see that just a few years later, mid-pandemic, I was ahead of the trend!

It's okay if others don't understand what you're doing, or how you have chosen to live your own creative life or run your own small business. We need to do these things because we're called to do them. I guarantee that this new found fire burning in your belly will be pretty hard to extinguish once you access it.

Let this flame guide you to glory. You deserve it. You really do.

FORK IN THE ROAD

Sometimes we choose to jump into a new creative path because of a fork in the road that presents two very clear paths. I want to encourage you to always explore the road less traveled. (I think I read that book, once).

As our dreams shift, sometimes ease can become more attractive to us. We might want to have a family or have other personal interests. Stability might become the desire. I understand this deeply, especially after the loss of a parent. The need for stability became my life source after my father passed. But I do want to encourage that if you're in a season of more flexibility and are brave enough to take the fork in the road, it might just lead to the most rewarding life.

My personal mantra in life is to do the hard stuff first so that I can take my time with the rest. I have never once opted for the easier path. Embrace the twists and turns, and flirt with the forks in the road. Follow your curiosity. Follow the work. Follow the opportunity.

YOUR CREATIVITY IS LIKE A FINGERPRINT

Your creativity and your creative process are like fingerprints—there is no one who will express themselves or navigate creativity exactly the way you do. Your creativity and the process in which you create are completely unique to you. This should bring you more relief because it allows for less judgement all around.

You'll notice as you start to execute additional visions or begin other creative ventures, that you will begin to have your own personal bottom line. This is good; this is what we strive for. This bottom line is what will serve you throughout this journey. This bottom line becomes part of your identity, and will inform many of the decisions, twists, and turns you'll choose to take.

MANTRAS AND MISSION STATEMENTS OR WHY AND WHAT FOR

These are important to have. Once we've acknowledged who we are and that we're moving forward in our creativity, we want to attempt to articulate this statement for ourselves and others. I like to call it my mantra, or intention. My mantra for the day is usually a private goal I set for myself that guides me through my handling of a project, or a state of mind that I might try to achieve throughout my creative process. Personally, I create the best when I link my mantra to a piece of my spirituality because I want my creativity to be a true reflection of my values. This is something that is extremely important to me. It's my bottom line.

Many of the artists I collaborate with like to call this a mission statement. You can usually find mission statements in the 'about' section of websites for most artistic companies or theatrical enterprises. When we have a mission statement, it helps us to organize our thoughts, and also informs others on who we are and what we do, and what we're actively working towards.

My dear friend and fellow multi-hyphenate, Michael Kushner, calls this the "why statement". If what you're creating doesn't match who you are or *why* you are doing it, then you're quickly able to see when something doesn't fit your brand or fall into place.

In college, my professor, Aubrey Berg, would pose the question "what for?" when we would talk about tactics and relationships in our junior acting class. What for do I do this? What for do I make this choice? Asking "what for?" informs us because it answers our deepest questions and, dare I say, *objectives*. So, what for are you starting this leg of your creativity? What for are you starting your new creative business? Or what for are you setting out on this journey?

Understanding your own mantra and bottom line is important because as we continue to expand into each project, series, or creation, we start to realize that each of these things can have their own mantra or mission statement, too. It's important to understand and to be able to state your intentions. That way, all of your ideas and choices can fall under a larger umbrella. The umbrella of you.

THE UMBRELLA OF YOU

Once we have uncovered that grounded sense of self from celebrating our creativity and authentic truth, let's begin the fun stuff. Let's claim our magic as the impetus to start our next project. Want to do a fun metaphoric exercise with me? I thought so!

I want you to imagine yourself standing in the middle of a field holding an umbrella. It's a beautiful day, so you might feel a little silly for holding it with the sun shining, but be proud of your state of readiness. Enjoy standing in the shade that you've created for yourself. The sun is shining, and although you don't need it quite yet, you're prepared. You know what you stand for. You know who you are and where you're going with that awesome umbrella of you.

The rain will come, but we're protected from it since we've created this sturdy and clear space. So when the rain comes, I want you to know that you will be ready for it. When the clouds begin to show their face and open up the sky, let the rain fall over your umbrella, your integrity, your message, and your truth.

Your umbrella is shaped like this for a reason. Let all of the raindrops fall over you. The pieces that don't fit. The pieces that don't feel like they should be a part of your new puzzle. Let all them wash over you (while you remain protected) and fall to the ground. You are the *only one* who can choose what belongs within the umbrella of you. Everything else? Let it go.

When we anticipate what might be ahead, we're ready for rainfall. And that state of readiness is a great place to be when starting something new. Now that you've taken in the moment, feel free to take your umbrella down and dance in the rain for a bit. A little dance in a sun shower never hurt anyone. But hold onto that umbrella, because we might have to use it later.

HUNGRY FOR STRUCTURE

Notice how things are starting to zone in a bit. You might be starting to have a little bit more clarity on where you're actually headed. I hope you have more confidence, too. The coolest thing about being an artist is that every single inch of you can become creative, even the part of having to be pragmatic to give yourself structure. There are massive amounts of creativity used when you step into the glorious "framing phase" to create your own structure. This is something I have grown to love.

We get to figure out what's best for you, what makes you soar, and how you will be most successful in your new creative venture. Remember, creativity is like a fingerprint, and when you allow yourself to create your own way, the possibilities for success in your future are truly endless.

CHALLENGES FOR PART ONE: IDENTITY

#BYOP CHALLENGE 1:
NO ONE CAN GIVE YOU PERMISSION TO CREATE BUT YOURSELF

1. In a journal or in your heart, describe how you are currently perceived as an artist. What do people come to see you do, perform, make, or create? How have you branded yourself? Are you known for anything specific? What steps have you taken to land yourself where you are today? Have you personally fueled this identity?

2. Sit in it. This is who you have shown yourself to be as an artist and how you have expressed who you are.

3. Do these things that you've written above match your current authentic truth? Is there something more that you need to say? Is there something further you need to explore? Is there some thought or energy that creates excitement in you?

4. If you can articulate them, jot those thoughts down.

#BYOP CHALLENGE 2:
REMAIN OPEN PAST FEAR

1. Do you have any current fears associated with your artistic output or creativity? Write them down.

2. Are these fears tangible? Are these fears rational? If so, why? Are these fears irrational? If you have some irrational fears like the rest of us, write those down on another page because they matter, but they aren't going to slow us down in our creative process.

3. If you had a new curiosity or idea pop into your head or heart during #BYOP Challenge 1, what are your fears associated with starting that project, lane of creativity, or expression?

4. Greet those fears, because as we turn the page, we're going to start to move towards them together. This time we are going to keep moving forward.

#BYOP CHALLENGE 3:
CELEBRATE YOUR ARTISTRY

1. Now that we are rocking our open artistic identities, where do you want to go?

2. Are there any artistic ideas or lanes that you once repressed? Write them down and celebrate them. Maybe you're onto something.

#BYOP CHALLENGE 4:
VALUE YOUR MAGIC

1. What gives you value? What do you value in yourself? What qualities do you have that are special about you as a person?

2. How are these gifts and skills used to create your magic? Is it in your creative method? Is your magic in how you relate to others? Is your magic found in being a pioneer, leading you down exciting and new creative paths? Write down your magic.

3. Look into your artistic and working relationships. Is there someone or something that has provoked you and makes you want to either protect or value your magic more? Meditate on these instances, or write those people down. These instances will inform us as we move forward, but they are not going to slow us down.

4. Sit in it. You have so much value, my creative friend.

#BYOP CHALLENGE 5: YOUR ARTISTS RECIPE

1. What environment do you best create in? Do you have to be alone to gather your thoughts with zero distraction? Do you have to be seated next to a group of people in order to feel motivated and on task? Do you prefer working from home?

2. What time of day works best for your workflow and creativity? Do you work better in the mornings? Do you prefer to only begin the crux of your work after the sun goes down? What time frame will give you the most creative consistency?

3. Does your creative working environment have to be kept tidy or do you prefer a little clutter? What must be taken care of physically in your environment in order for you to feel clear and focused?

4. How do you plan to deal with unexpected distractions throughout your work day? Will you tell your housemate you have scheduled working hours? Will you let your loved ones know the best time of day that they can reach you? What can you do to make your work flow the most consistent and uninterrupted?

5. Add these all together and you have your very own Artists Recipe! There is no right or wrong answer! This allows you to know what works for you and can become extremely helpful in further collaboration conversations.

#BYOP

PART TWO
INSPIRATION & THE IDEA

4

STARTING FROM SCRATCH

My favorite thing to do is to start something new. I love starting from scratch. You usually hear "starting from scratch" in terms of baking or cooking, and while my patience for the culinary arts is limited, it definitely isn't for the art that I feel at home in. I love to take all the time in the world and gently mix the ingredients to make my own (and others) art come to life. I love building, and I love strategy. A lot of my creativity comes straight from inspiration. I love experiencing that inspired feeling internally, and then outputting it and carrying it over into my art. That communication and expression is what makes me whole.

The inspiration materializes into an idea, and then it's up to me to mold it—to write, produce, sing, or act it—or maybe even present it in a format to readers like you. Like this book that you're reading!

I've never written a book before and didn't originally set out to write one. The inspiration came from my environment and the state of the world. It came from listening and trying to serve a needed purpose. #BYOP originally began as one-on-one consulting for producing projects, and encouraging people through creating their own work. As those teachings became more succinct, I had the opportunity to share them in a group setting by calling all creatives to a live stream class. It was then that I became inspired by the community. I asked our community what they were hungry for— what was something that might help them feel like they have more information or support at their fingertips? Then the idea came. *Oh! This inspiration should be translated into a book!*

Now, here's a really cool thing. Are you ready? (Can you tell these things excite me?) One of my favorite things to do is to feel inspiration and then figure out *how* it should be interpreted and shared. Meaning that as a creative, I'll have an experience or idea (or usually an emotion) that I feel is pretty rad and I feel called to express, but I don't know exactly how I should go about it. So, my question for you (with your very own inspiration) is this: what medium should you use to tell your story, or how should your story be told?

NON-DISCRIMINANT STORYTELLER

I am a 'non-discriminant' storyteller: a storyteller who tells a story in any way that inspiration may lead. You might see me up on a stage acting it, or off-stage directing it. You might read a story I've written, or see it in the form of a screenplay. You might see me create an environment so that other people can succeed in telling their stories. I tell stories. It's what I do as a creative. A fun part of my creative journey is that I never exactly know *how* I will be telling that story. It always changes job to job, or creation to creation.

I believe that each story has a certain medium where it can best be told. Not necessarily because of the subject matter, but because of how you want to translate it as the creative. How do you feel called to explore the subject? When you're starting from scratch, ask yourself this: what medium best serves the story? What medium best serves the audience's experience of the story? So, reader, this inspiration that you're feeling? That fire in your heart? What medium do you feel will best serve that story?

WHAT SERVES THE STORY

Let's take a look at what's inspiring you today so we can better understand how to craft the story you want to tell. Is it original? Was it inspired by existing content? Right off the bat these questions tell me so much when I'm speaking to creatives because it helps me to inform the structure.

I have a dear friend who came to me with an abundance of written journal entries. These entries would flow out of her with zero pull. In fact, they practically fell out! She felt that her journal entries might make a really powerful one-woman show, but because the subject matter was about personal and challenging events that happened throughout her life, she was afraid there might be a disconnect. We discussed this disconnect a lot.

We brainstormed different ways this story could be told, and in the end, she took my suggestion that instead of a one-woman show, she could make her journal entries into multiple monologues read by a cast of different women with the overall arc of the show still being her story.

THE COOL GIRLS

Here's one of my favorite stories of all time because it's what launched me into producing indie film and TV content. The story of *The Cool Girls,* or what became one of the first web series in the indie film world of New York City in 2013, *Rules of Cool.* I sat down with my best friend, Caitlin Cooke, and her roommate, Lacey Jeka, to look at a series of comedy sketches they wrote titled, *The Cool Girls.* There were about fourteen pages at the time, but inside these pages were a million ideas about two girls coming of age in their 20's in New York City. The main thing we wanted to do was to make this story accessible to people. *GIRLS* had just premiered on HBO and it was unearthing a new kind of gritty storytelling for millennials. With this in mind, we still thought there was plenty of room to share Caitlin and Lacey's stories, which were more vulnerable and goofier in comparison. They wanted the content to be a little more suited for high schoolers, should they stumble upon it on YouTube.

I looked at this series of sketches one afternoon at the Westway Diner with Caitlin, Lacey, and my buddy, Tracy, who was producing content for A&E at the time. (Pulling in Tracy was very important. We will come back to that in Chapter 6).

I started out by asking a lot of questions. How do you envision these sketches being done? Who do you feel should take part in telling them? Are there characters in these girls' lives that would make these sketches really come off the page? Who inspired you to write this? What characters could help this story to be told? Should your environment take on a role?

How this story should be told, or, what medium we should use to tell it, was found in the answer to these questions. We quickly realized that instead of just filming two girls alone on a stoop, talking about their daily mishaps and woes, that it would be more palpable and interesting to see them interacting with the people who got them there in the first place. This also allowed us to interact with the true star of the show, New York City.

We wanted to see the character of Lucy (played by Lacey) deal with her narcissistic ex-boyfriend. We wanted to meet the overly flamboyant neighbor, Norm, and watch him basically move into their small apartment. We wanted to see Joe, the landlord, get duped into coming to their party with zero guests, while they use him to take selfies and celebrate the "wild night they had" as he's crouched down fixing their sink. Such a wild party, right? And that became our pilot episode, *Throw a Party*.

I was so inspired by this set of comedy sketches and the potential of my colleagues and their story, that, in two-and-a-half hours, the four of us laid out what was to become season one of our new web series, *Rules of Cool*.

We used a crowdfunding site called Indiegogo and raised almost $13,000 in two months from family and friends. I pulled in the person who was to become my creative ride-or-die, Patryk Larney, and we shot the full season of *Rules of Cool* over four days in November. At the time, Patryk was mainly working in graphic design and band management, but he had great vision for this kind of thing. We also hired his buddy, Andy Strohl, who is one of the best cinematographers and editors I know. We shut down an entrance to Central Park, found a random bar in Brooklyn to shoot in, and offered some of our dearest friends a role. Finally, I navigated the emerging new media contract from SAG-AFTRA, which had just been created because of a new streaming platform you may have heard of called Netflix.

Rules of Cool was one of the most magical things I have ever been a part of. It was the cornerstone piece of AKA Studio Productions, and it was one of the first web series coming out of New York City. The only other group of creatives doing it at the time was a little show called *High Maintenance*. In late 2015, *Rules of Cool* was sold to a platform called Fullscreen, which was a subsidiary of YouTube Red. I actually negotiated that deal with my agent, Amy (who also encouraged me to write this book), while I was on set for probably my other biggest TV acting gig to date, *Unbreakable Kimmy Schmidt*. I always wondered if Tina Fey, the creator and executive producer of the show, knew I was creating my own work and that's why she gave me that job. In my heart and in that moment, I allowed myself to think that she did. I knew I'd found my calling by being on both sides of the camera at the same time, and knew that if I stuck with it, I would have endless access to inspiration.

IT CREATES ENERGY

If you're looking for a thumbs up or a green light for one of your personal inspirations or ideas... *ding!* You will get it from its energy. Does your idea create energy? With every project that I've moved forward with, I know one thing's for sure: it creates energy. That's how I know I'm on the right track.

When we began talking about *Rules of Cool* with people, they got excited. People would ask a bazillion questions. They'd ask how they could get involved, and most importantly, where they could see it. This also happened with our OG #BYOP client, Emm O' Connor, and her series, *Capital Advice*. People got excited about its logline, team, and story about Gwen, a DJ hailing from a small town trying to turn the world of local radio broadcasting on its head with her after-dark self-help program. This enthusiasm not only came from Emm, but also from her team. It came from her actors, from us, and it came from her supporters. *Capital Advice* got people excited and ended up being a huge success.

It was the same thing for our pilot, *Mulligan*. We had an important story, this time in the form of an hour-long drama series—one that really navigated the ins-and-outs of a city, and the struggles, triumphs, and resilience of the people of Pittsburgh. We realized in order for this pilot to be a success, we had to rally the entire city of Pittsburgh. And that's what we did. I'll share a bit more about this in Chapter 6 in the "Building Out from the Sides" section.

All of these projects created a massive amount of energy, and when you're creating your very own project from scratch, that's what you need: energy. Creating is hard, so you need to harness that energy in any way that you can. Energy becomes the momentum that your project thrives on, so we must cultivate it well, cherish it, protect it, and watch it reveal the next steps.

SOMETIMES INSPIRATION IS PLANTED AS A SEED

Before we move to take action on these inspirations and ideas, I want to remind you of one thing so you never discount something that you once realized a long time ago. Sometimes inspiration strikes, and you immediately know what actions to take; the path becomes clear, and you're ready to move. But sometimes inspiration can be planted as a quiet seed in your heart.

Have you ever been struck with an inspiration or experience that sticks with you, but you don't exactly know how to move forward with it? It's like an imaginary friend you might visit on a rainy day; it makes you feel good and connected when you say hello, but it's just there. You've obviously been inspired, but you don't exactly know what this inspiration or base idea is to become.

I don't want you to worry if you feel inspired but don't immediately act. Sometimes the most powerful inspirations need time to sit with you and marinate first, or sometimes they need an event or environmental change to actualize into a medium.

So, if there's something that might feel really big to you that you know you want to work towards, continue to visit with it. Continue to fill up your cup by living creatively and when the time is right, this inspiration will come back to you clearer than ever in the form of an idea that will be tangible.

INSPIRATION & THE IDEA COME HAND IN HAND

When I originally laid out this book, I had the inspiration and idea parts in different sections. What I realized, however, is that it's like the chicken and the egg; which actually comes first? I personally believe it's a form of inspiration that comes first, but usually a great idea isn't too far behind.

Once we get those ideas pumping through our veins is when the discipline and discernment must kick in to help us to organize and protect them. If we want these inspirations to actualize, we have to create structure for it. Period. As we're feeling inspired, things are going to narrow even more with our creativity because we're taking all of this hype (as our Multi-Hype group would say), energy, and momentum to lead us into action so all of our dreams can actually come true.

CAN I PICK YOUR BRAIN?

Yes, you can. No seriously, if you want to talk about your personal creativity with me after reading this book you can reach out to me and pick my brain about your amazing new idea. It's what started this whole thing and encouraged me to write this book. Our team is always down to be your own personal creative cheerleaders!

Whether it's me or somebody else that you trust, might I suggest picking *someone's* brain? When we start something new, we need help and support. If knowledge is available to you in the form of opportunity, relationships, research, and social media, then please, my creative friend, why don't you just go for it? We'll talk about the importance of relationships in the creative and small business world a bit later, but there's also something magical that comes with having knowledge on a subject.

I don't want you to stop yourself from taking action on an idea because of the lack of knowledge on something; you could be onto something completely original (it comes from you, so of course it is!). I'm asking you to always be open to learning. Remember that whole ego out the door thing? Always be open to being a student, *especially* if you are a leader. I'm going to just say that again. *Always be open to being a student, especially if you are a leader.*

I will forever be a student because every time I start something new, I am starting from scratch. As an artist this never goes away. I've performed on Broadway, and every time I start a new acting job, I say quietly to myself, *well I hope it comes out of me today!*

When we take action on our latest and greatest idea, we want to be prepared, confident, and informed, especially if we're leading in any capacity. It becomes your responsibility to help others to create with clarity. So, I want to challenge you to remain open to always learning more.

Knowledge is indeed power, and you can learn from experience as well as from study. You can learn from taking action or throwing yourself into a job. That's how I have gotten most of my artistic and creative education: by jumping in. Ask questions, pick people's brains, ask for guidance, and ask people to share their stories. I promise it will motivate you and help you. As Twyla Tharp wrote in one of her books (that I luckily picked up while in high school), *What's the worst thing that someone can say to you—? No?* But we know how to handle that. We let those no's roll over our umbrella of you, and right off of our shoulders. Sometimes we even use that no as fuel. I say it's time to light this sucker up!

5

IF NO ONE'S OFFERING YOU A CHAIR, BUILD YOUR OWN FREAKIN' TABLE

We're getting into the goods, my creative friend. The magic is starting to happen; I feel it bubbling and I'm ready to GO! I'm getting fired up. I'm choosing to curse because THIS IS IMPORTANT! Fellow creative, if there is one thing that you know in your heart you should be doing with your creative soul, but others aren't letting you partake in it, or they aren't inviting you to the table for it, you CAN build your own table. And if this is the circumstance that you find yourself in, I can almost guarantee you that you are supposed to be building your own table, and building it right *now*.

I'm going there because I can. I'm "going in" as I call it. Do you think that the great Lin Manuel Miranda ever asked someone permission to MAKE the room where it happens?! Absolutely not! He took personal action, inspired by his summer read of a book of public domain historical content. From that, he started building and navigating a larger than life musical concept with his teammates, workshopped and presented the content, perfected it for YEARS, and began building a brand that is still continuing to expand all day, errrrry day, 365 days a year (including the leap years).

Opportunity exists. You can create opportunity for yourself, but it will show up on your doorstep as work. Hard, hard, grueling work that will test you at almost every turn. This creativity thing ain't easy, especially if you want it to be your main source of income. But I promise you, it is possible, you just have to force yourself to grow, learn, navigate, and be more flexible and adaptable than ever before. I hope you picked up this book because you are ready. Sometimes it becomes more painful to not take action in your life and continue to sit idle than to try and create. You feel me?

Are you hurting? Let's get to work. Are you curious? Let's get to work. Are you tired of the rat race and still not being truly seen? Let's get to work! Everything you need is already inside you to build your own table, castle, and kingdom. You want to know the truth about the people who fall behind? They simply don't put in the work or push themselves to continue on their own journey.

GET ORGANIZED

We've arrived. It's time to get organized. I don't care how brilliant you are, if you aren't organized you will not be able to lead yourself or others effectively. Without being organized you might find yourself getting lucky once or twice, but more than likely it will be a flash in the pan, and then the sizzle will cease. If you are like me and are type A++, you have been patiently waiting for this moment;

your notebook, planner, and open google doc ready to go. Hello my people, you have come to the right place. If the past few sentences made you throw up in your mouth, then I hate to tell you, but you still need to grab a version of these tools anyway. I'm sorry, but you do.

When we are starting something new or creating in different ways, we have to gain others' trust. We can do this best by getting organized, creating consistency, and keeping a schedule.

CONSISTENCY IS KEY

Consistency is the key to everything. It is one of the clearest ways to build and gain forward momentum on your project. Consistency should be one of your main focuses as a creative if you are launching, rebirthing, or starting anything from scratch.

Here are some of my biggest thoughts of encouragement for you: do you know how many people have great ideas and inspirations? Do you know how many people wake up every day, have some of their greatest ideas, and allow themselves to get excited? Some people even take an action step or two. A bazillion every day. Now, how many of those bazillion creatives continue to remain consistent and actually follow through with their art, brand, or new small business idea? I guarantee you that this drops off to probably somewhere around 1%. This shouldn't discourage you; this should *encourage* you. Staying in it and being open to learning and setting new goals is *way* more than half the battle.

Consistency is something that is completely within your artistic and creative control. You can choose to wake up every day and do things to help yourself further your artistic journey. And remember, if you have been frustrated with that work/reward ratio that I spoke about earlier, creating your own work and creating your own way is something that you can always have a voice in.

EVERY DAY WE HAVE THREE CHOICES

I don't know how this came to me, but when I first moved to the big city, I knew that I was at the beginning of the largest career marathon of my life. You always hear as an actor, "If you can do anything else in the world, do it." People say this because it's grueling and difficult work, and 99% of the time, people simply don't have the room to work with you. They can only hire one person out of the thousands that are submitted for that one job. When moving to NYC, I knew I had a lot of groundwork to lay. I had a lot of people to meet and dues to pay, both literally and figuratively. I was hungry to start my journey, and I was eager to no longer be seen as green (I just wanted to get that part over with).

Something that helped me was to think that every day I have three choices: I can do the work to push myself forward in my career, choose to stay the same, or choose to take a step back. By taking a step back, I don't mean taking a mental health day or a week off, I mean make a stupid decision that takes time away from my broader goals at hand. For me in my early 20's, it could have been spending unproductive time somewhere (or with someone) or staying up/out way too late when I knew I had an audition the next morning and probably wouldn't do my best work.

DISCIPLINE

Your discipline *can* and *will* set you apart. This is a quality, that, if you have it, you know that no matter what that you have the ability to move yourself forward. It can become your safe guard. If you can make yourself show up every day to organize yourself, remain consistent, and get yourself ready to take action with your creativity, I promise there is no way that you won't move forward in this very uncertain world. Your discipline morphs into perseverance, which creates your own energy, almost like a generator. We want to be self-sustaining.

By implementing good habits, a schedule, understanding how you work best, and by respecting yourself, you're able to move and groove. And can I be honest? You just feel *better* about a lot of things. You deserve to live that good life, baby! If you hate being disciplined or consistent, might I suggest trying for an hour a day?

AN HOUR A DAY

This can serve you in starting anything new and scary. About three-and-a-half years ago in 2016, I started writing my first feature film screenplay. Other than a school project, I had never written anything before. It overwhelmed me to think about the final product and what I was working towards. I didn't truly understand the writer's structure, and I had no idea what screenplay software to use or where to even begin. But one thing that knew I could do for sure, was sit down and try. So, I did. I tried for an hour a day.

I first started by Googling "free screenwriting software," and also texted one of my former classmates, Lisa, who I knew had written a screenplay before. Once I figured that out, I started with the story, and what I understood within the puzzle of writing a screenplay. As an actor, I knew I understood dialogue, so that was my next step. Following that, I started to explore the story's structure.

Something magical started happening in this process, and I realized this is something I'd done in most of my other artistic lanes as well. The more I kept showing up, even at first for only an hour a day, the easier it became. And because it became easier for me to show up feeling like I could do it and write, my hour a day turned into two, which turned into three. From this, I also learned that I usually write best in 2-3-hour chunks.

As I'm sitting here writing this book, I'm writing it in 2-3-hour spurts. I have also found I work best in the morning. That's when content comes out of me the easiest—when I'm rested, when I'm calm, and when I feel the most connected. That's what I learned from working this way on my last writing project. I also write linearly! Weird, right? Oh, and I could never work in an office. I would waste so much time, and I could never focus. ANYONE ELSE?!

SAY YES SO THEN YOU CAN LEARN WHEN TO SAY NO

When starting something new, saying yes is a really solid way to begin. Want to collaborate with me? Yes. Will you sing at my cabaret that I can't pay you for, but is at a great venue? Yes. Can we sit in a coffee shop and strategize together? Yes. Do you want to take this audition appointment? Yes. Do you want to go to this random opening with me? Yes. At the beginning, or when we're starting something new or pivoting creatively, we need to attempt to say yes. It's how we build and show others that we're open to new opportunities, and how we create energy and momentum.

When I was first starting my acting career in New York City, I made a deal with the devil. The deal I made was to try to say yes to everything that came my way for the first five-year period, just to see what happens. And I did. One of my managers, the legendary Edie Robb who inspired the role of Joey's agent on Friends, wanted me to say yes so much that I hardly took a vacation. That never quite sat well with me, but what I tried to do was say yes to every business and social opportunity to lay my groundwork in the big city.

About a year in came my first big crash. Because I was saying yes so much, I was spent. My entire life I had been go, go, go up to that point. From my performing arts high school, to a very demanding musical theatre college program, to working professionally during my summers off and moving to New York, getting my agent and manager, and just... working, working, working. And by working, I mean performing, auditioning, babysitting, cocktail waitressing and more, on repeat. In my entire life, I had never learned how to rest properly. I had no clue what self-care was. I was constantly living in survival mode.

After one year of living in the big city, my anxiety began. I'm from Kentucky, and was raised there in the 90's... Anxiety, what? Come again? Because it's beyond important, taking care of yourself is getting its own chapter a bit later, but for right now at this part of my story, I just need you to understand that because of my people pleasing issue and saying yes, I was on empty.

I was in the middle of filming my first movie, which, to put kindly, was psychological warfare. I flew to New York to do a reading of a new musical on my week off from filming, and while I was at that reading, on my lunch break I went to a callback in the same building for *Bring It On: The Broadway Musical*. I had nothing left in me. It was too much, and I wasn't taking care of myself at all because I hadn't learned how to yet. I was a green actress, raised in a people-pleasing "good-girl" culture, and it was truly messing me up and running me into the ground.

And then I had a panic attack in the lobby of Manhattan Theatre Club. That's when everything exploded. Classy, right? I didn't even know what a panic attack was. I was 22-years-old, living by myself in New York City, and I hadn't even heard of that term! I thought I was dying. I didn't know what to say, or who to tell, or even how to begin to describe it. I remember walking out of the rehearsal room and passing Alicia Silverstone (one of my idols!) as I tried to calm myself down outside on a bench. It was bad. I had no idea how to find my way out of the moment. I didn't even know where to begin.

The reading I was doing happened to be directed by the gentle visionary, Brian Yorkey. His show, *Next to Normal*, had just exploded onto Broadway, making history by creating the next level of musical theater storytelling. He had also just won a Pulitzer Prize for the show. Post panic attack, Brian called me up to his desk (a simple fold-up table) and asked me how I was doing. The timing couldn't have been more perfect. Now, envision my blank face. I couldn't believe it. *Either I have a massive target on my head or this guy is actually paying attention and cares about my well-being.*

I was—mostly—honest with him, and trying to radiate that I wasn't going to be a problem. But secretly, I was struggling to keep up all of my responsibilities at once. I was putting so much pressure on myself to seem perfect when, in reality, I was brand new to the industry, doing really challenging things, and working on some important projects with zero tools on how to take care of myself. The amount of pressure I was putting on myself was insane, even within this small exchange.

He studied me effortlessly and simply said, "Sometimes you have to learn to say no. You have to learn to take care of yourself or you'll drive yourself crazy."

Brian was correct. He was right on the money. I felt seen without explanation. I felt heard while screaming inside. I kept repeating that to myself throughout the day, playing it like a broken record. *I have to learn how to say no.* And the saddest part was that at the time, I didn't think I had the right to say no in my own life. From that day on, I set off on a journey to learn how to say no. And to tell you the truth, a decade later, I'm still learning how to do it (although I've gotten a lot better at it). It always makes me feel uncomfortable, but I know I have to do it or I can't be of service to myself and others productively.

I've always wanted to thank Brian for this moment of seeing me when I was so young, so this is my thank you. With his advice, I've learned to get better at saying no. Brian then went on to create the television series, *13 Reasons Why* for Netflix. He has such a special ability to really connect with young people and help them tell their stories of struggle and finding their way.

It's important for me to share this story with you because becoming my own producer is what gave me the confidence and ability to be able to start saying no. Running my own production company made me feel like I was working towards a larger picture, and also helped me deeply with my own personal (very private) self-worth. It took having some success in producing to gain the courage to tell my acting agent that I think we should pass for the first time. I had to start passing on some things because I knew that at the end of the day I wouldn't be able to make room for the things that made me want to say 100% YES!

BUSINESS SAVVY?

So, are you ready to take your organization to the next level? When I was starting to build my own production company, it didn't immediately click with me that I was starting my own business. If you create anything (an idea, product, or service), and you intend to sell it or set a ticket price, you are starting your own small business.

I was always so intrigued by the phrase "show business", and that's exactly what this creative industry is! It's a *business*, and we have to guard our art and acknowledge it as such.

Now, when you're just starting out with your small creative business, you don't have to have your own LLC. LLC stands for Limited Liability Company, and it costs a lot of money to file and register with the state. An LLC or partnership is a wonderful thing to do if you have multiple business partners in a singular entity. If you're not ready for this larger step, what is most important is that you do claim your business as an actual entity, but there can be a much more accessible option depending on what state you are in.

Look into registering yourself as DBA (Doing Business As), also known as a Sole Proprietorship. It has almost the same structure as an LLC, but many times it's not as expensive. Becoming a DBA is a great choice if you are personally offering your services without salaried employees, but you're ready to become more serious about your business. Many don't know about this, but if you're an LLC with only one member (like some independent producers or production companies) you actually file your taxes the same way!

It's important to file with the state because you want to be able to be recognized. You'll be recognized when doing creative business, and also by your books. By having a DBA or an LLC, you're able to acknowledge your business expenses—and as artists, we're always investing in our art. If you purchase supplies for a painting you plan to sell, or ingredients to bake a cake for your bakery, these are all known as expenses.

If you're producing a short film and you pay to rent the space or purchase props and costumes, these are all expenses! You can write these things off. They are an expense of your business the same way a real estate company might write off the expense of printing advertisements or yard signs. These expenses should be kept in their own spreadsheet. I recommend Google Docs if you don't want to pay for QuickBooks. It works just as well!

When you pay an employee, intern, or actor who works on your property, those are also expenses. You need to keep track of these things because the people or employees who are paid over $600 will need a 1099 at the end of the year. You must do this if you're claiming their payment as a business expense because you have to be able to show the track of that expense to the government if you are ever audited.

I know I might sound like a nut, but keeping track of these business matters can become fun. Like everything, starting something new can become easily exhausting because you're using so much adaptive energy to learn how to do it. I want to encourage you to keep going because I promise you, just like trying something for an hour a day, it *will* become easier for you! Every year I show up more prepared to do my taxes and I will tell you one thing: it's a massive relief. It's also something I'm very proud of.

Take the time and register your creative entity to protect yourself. Don't let this slow you down, but when you're building, make sure to take the time to acknowledge these steps. They are very important steps that, at times, might feel frustrating or boring, but it's extremely important to be prepared.

MISSION POSSIBLE

You're noticing this is challenging, right? To live as authentically as we can with our creativity and to create our structure accordingly? Though I also hope this journey is empowering you. I hope the stories above are opening your heart, and also showing you that with hard work, focus, and intention, all of this is within your power of choice and control. We just have to tread lightly, take our time, continue to listen, and sometimes make extremely hard choices. But by doing all of this, we *will* move forward.

Now that we've had a moment of talking about some of the hard stuff, do you want to know one of the best parts about building your own table? You get to give others a seat and invite them to *your* party. It's time to build your tribe! And this time, you get to choose who gets an invitation!

6

YOU CAN DO ALL THINGS, BUT YOU CAN'T DO THEM ALONE

You truly can do all things, but if you think you will achieve them and reach that brilliance completely alone, locked away in a room somewhere with only you and your brilliant self, boy do you have another thing coming! We are only human. When creating, we have to have life experience, stimulation, and support to get these stories out of us, even when we're telling our own.

Other people and fellow creatives can be our lifeline. On your own you can help ground a project or a creative idea, but pretty soon your team of one will need to grow. Your team can include anyone who is important to you. It can be a friend who might encourage you to keep moving forward, a parent or partner who you trust with information, or a colleague, business partner, collaborator, or employee.

These people should be brought into your circle with some very important things kept in mind. Do you remember in Chapter 3 where we talked about our bottom lines, mission statements, and mantras? These people who you invite to your party should match the hopes, dreams, visions, and goals that you have. What you're working towards as a team will become something sacred that we hope everyone will respect and work hard together to uncover.

Sometimes life happens. Sometimes by chance we meet someone who will become our "ride or die" collaborator or friend, or we stumble upon someone on Instagram who might change the course of our lives or career path. Sometimes the opposite happens and people cling to us—we can't quite understand why, but it never feels completely comfortable.

In this chapter, we're going to talk about some of those personality types, skill sets, and scenarios. One of the main reasons I wanted to write this book was to help you defuse fear and better navigate your creativity, but also to help debunk collaboration. At some point, these two things usually come hand in hand. Let's take our time. Remember, it's okay to take some time when welcoming someone onto your team.

BUILDING OUT FROM THE SIDES

People hold a lot of power. I'm talking a massive amount. And I'm not talking about the idea of a studio or network head, I mean working creatives just like us hold massive amounts of power, because together, we hold massive amounts of possibility. So far on our journey we've discovered that our creative ideas hold a lot of power, magic, and energy. Just imagine what happens when more than one of us get together and set our minds to a common goal? That energy expands and multiplies! This energy, quite frankly, can become palpable. Thoughts and action steps can become clearer, and now you have not one, but two (or even three) creative hearts, minds, and spirits hard at work.

When I start a new project or begin to expand on a creative idea, I call the act of bringing on fellow creatives, "building out from the sides". It can be one of the most important parts because as you build out from the sides, you are creating an army: a front line of creative soldiers who are willing to build with you, walk with you, and to move forward with you. Instead of standing alone, screaming and waving your arms in what feels to be a big open field, you now have a team standing with you and walking forward with you, step by step.

It's a powerful image, right? A massive group of people walking forward towards you in slow motion? Like the witches from *The Craft*, the fabulous four walking into battle, or heck, even *The Babysitters Club!* There's power in a group because there's more energy, but we want to make sure it's good energy. We want to protect it.

Sometimes we have to build out from the sides strategically. There are people who might have more awareness or experience than you in certain lanes of development, collaboration, or production. These are the perfect people to build out from the sides with because they'll bring you support and confidence with their very own expertise!

When I was starting to look into *Rules of Cool,* I knew I needed to get someone on the team who had the experience of network development and awareness. Although I was up for all of the building and learning, I needed guidance from a more dialed in party.

For this project, I chose to build out from the sides with my friend Tracy Goldenberg. She had worked for A&E and was aware of the expectations of developing content at a network level. She taught me how to break down a script, and trained me on how to make a shooting schedule that could work with our budget.

With indie projects, if you're looking to perform or shoot something on location, sometimes you have to build out from the sides within that area. We did this with *Mulligan*. We knew if we didn't have support from the city of Pittsburgh, we wouldn't be able to create a successful television pilot there. Everyone needs a team, and the more team members you can build out from the sides with, the more your project will feel supported and begin to creatively levitate into action!

BASIC INSTINCT

Sometimes when I'm producing, I use my history to inform some creative decisions. There are some people who flat out inspire me. I may have worked with them as actors in the beginning of my career, or started collaborating with them when I was younger. Eric Nelsen is one of these people. Eric is a multi-Emmy winning producer, and Drama Desk and Tony nominated producer with his beautiful and amazing wife, Sainty Nelsen. You may know Sainty from FX's *Sex & Drugs & Rock & Roll,* or as the voice of Nova Swift from *Trolls: The Beat Goes On!* Both have backgrounds in acting, and we all started producing and creating in new lanes around the same time. When my creativity output started to change, I knew right away that Eric was a person I had to create with. He inspired me, and I wanted to feature him as an actor because I felt his talent could shift into any medium and style. Not to mention he is an amazing human, and those things matter the *most*, my people.

Eric and I spoke about many projects, but the first one where I truly got to see him in action was when he expanded a role in Diana Amsterdam's play, *The Dodgers*. We knew we wanted to develop the play further out in Los Angeles, and Eric was already there to focus on his film and TV career. We also knew he had a theatrical background because he grew up in New York City, and starred in the Broadway musical, *13*. With the support of our trailblazing casting director, Daryl Eisenberg, and with me cheering Eric on from the sidelines, the choice felt like a no-brainer.

Eric flourished in the role of Chili, making him an unforgettable part of the show. He nurtured the role and elevated the play, and also, because he's a dream to collaborate with, he was the perfect choice to build out from the sides with.

Post-play, Eric inspired a role in the creation of our short film, *Ace*, a role in a film that was inspired by my life called *Beauty Mark,* and he was also someone who inspired me to write one of the lead characters in my feature film, *Boy Hero*. Sometimes the gut just knows and instinct takes over, allowing us to continue working together. And even today, I'm deeply looking forward to the next time we get to collaborate.

COME UP TOGETHER

I've got another example for you: the collaboration with my creative brother, Patryk Larney of Hope Tree Entertainment. Patryk and I met almost nine years ago and have collaborated on at least half of everything I've produced in my career of creativity.

We met one night at our friend Rachel Potter's concert at Joe's Pub, the music venue attached to the Public Theatre (the company that developed a little show called *Hamilton)*. Patryk was helping develop and package Rachel's country crossover career, working on her digital presence, taking pictures, and helping to package and push her forward. I was just being a helpful friend and passing out digital downloads for them at the door, but Patryk and I immediately clicked.

We kept in touch, and the first few of our collaborative meetings were about my songwriting at his old house in Brooklyn. We would banter and update each other about the projects we were working on and the people we were making things with. Then our opportunity came. Or well, let's be honest—we created it. Patryk had a genius mind for branding and a gift for visual presentation. He also had a background in music, and at the time, he was managing another girl duo, The Vanity Belles, who had one of the *best* album covers I have ever seen to this day. That album cover also happened to be created by Patryk.

One day, my father picked up the phone to tell me about a band he'd discovered that was based in Southern Indiana called The Hart Strings. They were an awesome Mumford & Sons type trio (who happened to be teenagers who played string instruments) that packed a lot of potential. To get these Indiana high school kids some exposure and help develop their brand and base, I knew we had to do some outside of the box thinking. So, I asked Patryk if he would be interested in developing a music video treatment for their first single, *Sharp*. He did, and it was fabulous. The video turned out great, served an awesome purpose of introducing the band to a larger audience, and helped them make it to the final round to open for CBS's #GRAMMY Gig Awards (a live taped pre-show for the GRAMMYs). Next, we landed the boys a record deal with New York label, Razor and Tie.

The catch was that because the boys were still in high school, their parents weren't ready for them to take off in their professional careers. But Patryk and I saw the potential and we were, so we stuck together. Next, we collaborated on *Rules of Cool*, the project that helped launch my production company, AKA Studio Productions. Patryk directed it, and we worked together on all of the marketing. He knew how to pull off a glorious music video, so why couldn't he soar at telling a narrative story with dialogue? A little different, but a similar kind of storytelling skill set. Both mediums are on camera, and both mediums expanded greatly with the support of a larger team.

From that moment on, Patryk became my visual and digital collaborator. He is the person I bring on for all my content for the larger projects. We've collaborated on the development of The Hart Strings, *Rules of Cool, The Dodgers,* #BYOP, and now he's helping me to develop the campaign for *Boy Hero*. I can verbally state what's in my mind for movie posters, pitch decks, graphic ideas and video edits, and Patryk makes it a reality. He even designed this book cover! Pretty snazzy, right? It's actually because of him that I was introduced to my financial advisor, Jeff Hammer, who then introduced me to the publishers over at Morgan James!

Patryk is now based in Nashville and managing some large musical acts like his fiancée, the stunning Liz Longley, and the limitless country duo, The Young Fables. He also collaborates and develops many other artists and artistic identities, not to mention he runs his own independent music festival every year called BUFF-STOCK. A decade later, we are still collaborating almost every day, but now we're both growing and hitting a bit of a stride in our creative careers. We have come up together.

You can do this, too, with your potential collaborators. You can build lifelong teammates, but it takes time, loyalty, listening, and open collaboration. We choose who to invest in when we build our teams. Patryk was a correct investment of my time, energy, and budget funds. We have continued to come up together as a team, and are now among each other's best creative confidants and friends.

It takes a lot of trust to build these types of bonds that can last and withstand all of the crazy flows of the entertainment industry, but it is possible. Always keep the door open for these kinds of people who come into your life and have helped you to create energy. Try to find spots for them, try to give them opportunities to collaborate and have their creative voice heard. In most cases, these people will treasure what you've built together and will have your back.

Now, can you imagine your collaborators also creating their own network and army throughout the years? That energy is boundless, which means the possibility and shelf life of those collaborations will be never ending. Building out from the sides is truly how you can make a creative project or life flourish. Your team is everything, and can be your make or break. We must choose wisely.

CAN I TAKE YOU TO COFFEE?

This is one of the most popular and powerful questions in the creative industry. It's usually the one asked before two highly creative, driven, and focused people sit down to create some magic, and, as I like to say with my favorite collaborators, "scandal and scheme". It's also an incredible way to ask advice and develop deeper creative and collaborative relationships.

One of the most important coffee meetings of my life was with Daryl Eisenberg, who at the time, was trailblazing as the youngest casting director on the scene in New York City. To me, she was— and still is—the epitome of a #GIRLBOSS. She never spoke about her age towards the beginning of her career, but I think when we first sat down together as two driven female collaborators, we were both in our early 20's. Daryl had given me my fist big role out of college in *The Gay Bride of Frankenstein,* and truly fought for actors like something I had never seen before.

I graduated into the commercial world of musical theatre at the same time as all of the cast members of reality TV competition shows like *Grease: You're The One That I Want.* Because of the popularity of these shows, I often found myself in final callbacks with the people who were on them for large acting opportunities, making it down to the final two, and being told "you're *not* the one that we want." But for *Gay Bride*, Daryl fought for me. So, as I was called to start producing and open my own production company, I felt like she would fight for me in that lane too. And she did.

She asked me about my fears, and we talked about being young women and wanting to make our own things. I didn't have many examples other than her to show that it was even possible. She was so poised and encouraging when I asked her how to start, and looked at me point blank and said, "you just do it." She encouraged me that there would be a team of people behind me with every project, and if I ever had any burning questions, I could always come to her. So, in that moment I took an action step to get her involved. It's so sweet to think about now that I asked her to be on my "board of wisdom".

I had never led anything before, and when I first started, I didn't know why anyone would trust me with their creative ideas, hopes, and dreams. I made a board that consisted of Daryl, Billy Butler, the composer of *Gay Bride*, and Christophe Caballero, the dance captain from *La Cage*. They were all creatives who I believed in and returned the favor, and because they believed in me, I had the courage to jump off and create something new.

Daryl is still someone I call on to this day. Sometimes I even have the opportunity to hire her to cast my own projects. She has continued to cheerlead my acting career (and probably offered me a fourth of it). My favorite Daryl story is when she was giving birth to her first son; she was literally drafting offers with our team for *The Dodgers* as she was going into labor. I treasure Daryl, the working relationship and friendship we've had over the years, and what she gave to me on that first coffee date together, which was confidence.

Who is in your circle that you should be asking to coffee in person or virtually? Who are you dying to hear more about or feel might be able to give you some really solid advice? Who do you see a bit of yourself in? Who are you hungry to collaborate with? Maybe asking for a bit of their time might just be the boost you need. And hey, that meeting could be the start of a lifelong creative teammate and collaboration.

THIS IS A RELATIONSHIP-BASED BUSINESS

The entertainment industry is both a relationship-based business and a business of creative collaboration. I won't even begin to take credit for that. It was taught to me by another influential creative in my life, the great Krisha Bullock. Krisha has cast some of the most popular Nickelodeon shows on television, and helped to launch careers like Ariana Grande, Jordan Fisher, Liz Gillies, and Jace Norman from *Henry Danger*. She also happens to be a huge fan of my buddy, Eric Nelsen, who I mentioned at the top of this chapter. This perfectly ties back to her statement that this is indeed a relationship-based business.

There is the traditional route of the industry where there is a mighty structure, loopholes, and dues to pay. But there is also magic that is assisting you from the sides. These are your relationships, so you MUST take good care of them.

Doing this whole creativity thing for a career at times can feel nothing short of brutal, but it's the people in those relationships that you have the opportunity to nurture and collaborate with who will always be rooting for you. They invest in you, they are the people who will push for you, pick up the phone for you, and collaborate with you along the way.

When you look at the people around you right now creatively, look at all of the possibilities of lanes, introductions, and collaborations that might be possible based on those relationships. Many of these people might become instrumental to you and your journey if you further develop those relationships; if you show up for them, support them, engage them in conversation, or offer your help or services.

Because of our relationship, after I'd assisted her classes many times when she visited the east coast, Krisha saved my butt big time when we had a project shooting on the west coast. Eric, who had booked another larger job, had to be replaced last minute on our film. I asked her if she could come on to help us, and she brought her entire office onboard. She cast the film in about 48-hours' time, and has been a cheerleader for me personally and creatively ever since. A relationship-based business, indeed.

SISTERHOOD OF THE CRAZY IDEAS

If you're a young woman reading this book, I want to take a moment to give you your own little version of a #BYOP Challenge. As women in the creative arts (or in any field for that matter) we MUST help each other along. We must fight for each other and give each other more opportunities to be heard.

I am proudly a member of many sisterhoods, both personally and creatively, and many of the women in my life are a part of both circles. I ask you to expand the circle. There is no group more unstoppable than a group of aligned women.

At my production company, we try to focus on creating these opportunities. There are plenty of articles about the film industry saying that only so much content is created, directed, or shot by women, so we decided that we needed to put our choices where our mouth is.

This is a relationship-based business, so remember that when you are making choices, you might need to develop some new relationships to help the cause. There are ways to engage with creatives in your circle and also create more opportunities for women.

Other young women have been my champions in the industry, but I would be cutting out the fat if I didn't mention some older women who have been challenging towards me. I don't fault them for having that initial instinct, and I understand that the world (and specifically our country) was structured differently when they were younger and didn't allow many opportunities for young women to lead. At some point though, we have to hold these other women accountable in the most loving ways.

All of this is to say that when people are not kind or encouraging to you, try to meet them with boundaries and patience. Some people are not going to be fans of yours, and it has absolutely nothing to do with you. When it's a gut instinct from someone to whom you've shown no malicious harm, you have to accept that it's just something that might have to exist within that creative or working relationship. Guard your heart, use your voice, and do not let a struggling personality steamroll you.

It will be challenging, but try to meet these people with grace for the sake of your team, what you are trying to accomplish creatively, and for your heart. It will be exhausting, but at the end of the day you will be proud of how you handled yourself. It can't always be rainbows and butterflies, but the goal is to be able to fall asleep at night with ease.

WHEN PEOPLE REPEAT, YOU ARE IN THE RIGHT PLACE

Repetition is truly an amazing thing. Have you ever been thinking about someone and out of the blue they just appear? Or you're curious about collaborating with a person who is new to you, so you begin to research them and suddenly you see them everywhere? Or those times when you keep hearing someone's name over and over? This is usually a good sign.

Usually the best kinds of people find their way to each other. You are not only perceived by your own actions, but also by the company you keep. At some point, the people who collaborate with you become an extension of you. If you're sharing a creative property together, they become an extension of the idea. They also represent you, so you need to choose wisely.

When people start to repeat, you know you're on the right track. It's a high five from the universe letting you know you're in good company. Do the research on people and see what their previous creative and working relationships are. It's more than likely if they've collaborated with people that you trust multiple times, they might just be a good fit for you.

TEAM UP WITH DIFFERENT GIFTS

Hire with your needs in mind. We cannot do it all alone. As independent creatives, contractors, and business owners, we know there aren't enough hours in a day, so I encourage you to ask people who might have a different skill set than you to join your team.

Now these people with different gifts than you still have to share your same common goals, but it's a good thing if they might have a different idea on how to achieve that same goal. That's what you want. Of course, you want people you can delegate to, but you also need people to work and collaborate with who have independent minds. You want to work with people who are thinking of the big picture—people who will ask questions and hold you accountable, and most importantly, will speak up when their idea is more efficient than your own. This is what you should hope for.

If you're just starting to branch out into employee land, and are worried about pay as you try to expand your team... Hello! Interns do exist. This is the number one suggestion I try to give my clients who are starting to flounder. It's hard to learn how to delegate and let go of your creative baby a bit, but sometimes it's completely necessary to move forward and expand.

When you sit down to bring anyone on your team, that's some serious reflective work. This process can be so good for you and your creative entity or small business idea. When you create or share work with others, you have to share what you cannot handle or what someone else might do more efficiently. Personally, I love making graphics. It's one of my favorite things; to embrace that direct-to-consumer experience. But right now, I have to focus on this book or there won't be any reasons to make graphics. Do you see what I mean? You can bring people to your team who work faster than you in those specific areas.

Delegation helps to create fluidity, brain space for thinking, and strategy (which we need). With great people by our side, there is no choice but to expand.

TAKE YOUR TIME

When it comes to expanding, I know internally you feel like a rocket ship ready to take off, but the most important thing to do is to take your time. When we choose who to align with for our creative and small business adventures, we need to give ourselves a moment for discovery, introduction, and reflection.

I know this is hard to believe, but anyone can pretend to be the correct fit for a creative job opportunity. People can present themselves in certain ways within their own excitement, but what we're looking for is consistency in them. What can you count on them for when the going gets tough? What can you actually expect from them when the relationship becomes comfortable?

There is a lot of pulling rabbits out of thin air within launching a creative entity or idea to a mass audience. I want to encourage you to take your time when looking into expanding your team. Reflect on it. Take that time from the discovery phase, and observe where the person has been, their history, and where they're going. Do their larger dreams align with yours? Are you all heading in a similar direction? Are they game to be a true support to you through thick and thin? Through the really exciting, easy stuff, and all of the million bumps ahead in the road?

I promise you the right ones will give you an appropriate amount of time to reflect. Sit with the idea of them, the idea of being in contact with them all of the time, because that is what these things tend to grow to whether they are a business partner, distributor, or collaborator of your art.

You are worthy of taking that time.

IMPRESSIONS OF OTHERS & DO THEY ALIGN?

When we meet with people that we might potentially collaborate with, we usually tend to focus deeply on how we present ourselves during a meeting or a Zoom call so that they want to come work with us. We have the tendency to want people to like us, and for people to want to come on board for our latest and greatest idea. What I would like to encourage you to do as you expand your creative ventures is to flip that thinking. I want you to focus on the impression of *others*, and encourage you to think about the person who is wanting to join your team. Ask yourself, why? Did this person reach out to you directly? Did they come recommended? Did they respond to a job posting somewhere, or have they been following your work for a little while? What is your impression of them? If it's a blind meeting, I encourage you to be aware of that, and allow that to inform your questions. You want to get to the bottom of why they feel called to be with you at this meeting. You also want to focus on this person's track record of action as well as their intentions.

When we conduct an interview, it's easy to be overtaken by someone's presentation and words. It's much more challenging to remain consistent and hold down an opportunity than it is to present yourself in a certain way for thirty minutes to get a job. Try to get to know where this person is from and what their history is. How have they moved forward in their career? Where have they been and where do they hope to go? Do their dreams align with yours? If we don't take the time to address these questions, when things begin to shift, it's usually because one of these points wasn't discussed in the first place.

Personal recommendations and existing relationships are my absolute favorite way to build my teams because there's already a bit of trust there. If you worked well with a person, and then that person highly recommends someone else for a freelance opportunity or position, nine times out of ten it's probably going to be a great fit. Now, there is that one out of ten times where I'll admit that I moved too fast in business with a blind recommendation. Take the recommendation into account, but still be sure to put the work in to make sure this is the right kind of human for you to be teaming up with.

What you have to ask yourself is this: does this person align with your own personal brand? Does this person align with the way you present yourself? Would this person align well with the rest of your team? And do you feel like this person could be a good representation of you? If your name is on the gig, that person is an extension of you. I don't care how large or small the opportunity might be. Ask yourself this: is this person a true extension of myself?

"BUSINESS BOMBERS" BEWARE

When we don't take our time, sometimes really bad things can happen. I call this "business bombers" beware! Have you ever been in one of those romantic relationships that just moved way too fast? Like zero to one hundred overnight? Mmmhm. Me too. When you look back on it with a rational mind, everything seems like a blur and you wonder how it actually happened in the first place. If all signs point to yes, you might have been in a relationship with a "love bomber".

Well, my friends, this can happen with our artistic businesses and creations too. This type of evil creeps in by way of latching onto our ego. Have you ever had someone just cling to you or your ideas and act like you just unlocked their world? I'm not talking about a person you've known of or spoken to consistently over a certain period of time, I'm talking about a brand-new person that you don't know from Adam. Now, it's tricky because a little bit of this is good, but you're ultimately looking for teammates who are able to add you and your project into their existence, not make their entire existence your project. I say this because there might be many ulterior motives to this.

Our art and our platforms, to us, are like what can be found in a banker's vault. They should be held and kept sacred. I know it's hard to even think about our art in relation to money, but we must protect it the same way we do money. We are all here meeting through the pages of this book because we hope to possibly make our living, or a portion of it, from our art or creativity. So, value that. Value your ideas, your history, your time and your relationships. A random person who you barely know doesn't get to tell you things they know you want to hear for a few days (or even in a single conversation—yes, I have made this giant misstep before) and expect you to just hand over the keys to your castle. I have been there. I have let those types of business bomber personalities come into my creative work and business and blow everything up like a bomb. It is completely decimating. And if you only remember one thing from this entire book, remember this: take your time to get to know your collaborators before you begin to work with them. Look into them. Ask about them. Look into their history. Have they remained consistent? How does their reputation precede them? Because that reputation is about to become yours.

LOVE YOUR TRIBE

Other humans are necessary for collaboration and expansion of our very own sacred and creative ideas, but they can truly be the make-or-break to our next destination. Take your time getting to know the people you choose to bring onto your team. At the end of the day, this really boils down to how you navigate valuing yourself and your business. Remember, we don't need anyone to come and save us, everything we need is already inside us to achieve all of our wildest dreams.

When we take our time to create the right kind of tribe, we can then follow them wherever they may go. Those people with whom you make a conscious decision to invest your time, ideas, and resources into will never forget that vulnerability and openness. Love your tribe and love them hard. They will be the ones who hold you above the water, project to project, through the ups and downs of the industry, and be there to catch you when life happens.

7

GOOD OL' IMPOSTER SYNDROME

So, this incredible idea you have is starting to take on a life of its own, right? It's probably even a bit different than you imagined. As you move along your creative journey, you'll start to notice more holes, twists, and turns than you even thought were possible. Welcome to the joys of starting something new. This is the murky navigation of make-or-break that forces us to show up every day and be unapologetic about our dream. Without it, everything would just stop dead in the water. When all of the pieces are together and everything is primed and ready to take off, your confidence might begin to falter. But have no fear, a little turbulence doesn't mean we're headed for a complete disaster.

All of this work you've done leading up to this point might feel like it's never going to be enough. Based on one conversation with a mentor you might begin to question every piece of your path, declare your strategy is a hoax, or decide you'll never quite reach that celebration of a big launch.

I will now ask you to imagine me entering the stage dressed in some black and white *Victor/Victoria* style costume, complete with top hat, as I summon the curtains to open. The audience cheers, and written in bright bulbs behind the parting, luscious red curtain, are those wonderful words *Good Ol' Imposter Syndrome* (takes bow).

Welcome! You have arrived at the mecca of the creative process! You have reached the classic benchmark of creating something new or blasting off into stardom: *imposter syndrome!* We must accept and embrace it, because we need this little demon to visit us and exit the stage door as quickly from whence it came!

WHY ME?

Well, because, why not? You have this authentic, creative idea that I bet was inspired by your history, your deepest hopes and dreams, and/or your personal vision for your future. You have this idea, and you've done all of this work because it's you who is supposed to carry the torch—Olympic style—to your final destination and holy grail.

You are special enough to have this idea! The idea or creative entity wouldn't even be a thing without you. I know I haven't been talking to a wall for the last 100 pages. You are the magical piece to this puzzle. No one else.

I get asked "why me?" a lot from colleagues and brilliant #BYOP clients calling to ask for advice. Why, you might ask? Because you had the ability to dream this, plan it out, and take action on it, that's why! It goes back to that whole statement, "if you can dream it, you can do it".

I've also asked myself "why me?" throughout my own creative journey. I ask myself this just as much when things are going right, as when they're going wrong. I've asked myself why I set out to create my own production company as a young female with hardly any experience in a male dominated industry. *Why couldn't you have just wanted one creative lane in your life and had a bazillion less responsibilities than some actors or people who seem to have a lot more flexible time on their hands?* But the secret answer is that I was called to do this, just as you were too.

We were called to be where we have arrived today. Point blank. And you wouldn't have found yourself here, flipping through the pages of this book, if you weren't meant to be. You created this idea, this space, this magic, and so it is yours to have.

IF YOU MADE THE ROOM, IT'S YOURS

Read that again. It will give you some fuzzies. That's right: *if you made the room, it's yours.* If you are the human who cultivated this idea, team, event, or production for people to rally and gather around, it is *yours*.

My brave creators who make a web series or write a play that's getting ready for its first table read will say to me, "Oh my God, I just can't believe everyone will be there, looking at me, asking me what's next or expecting me to lead them to the next moment!"

Yes, you are *that* cool! You are the *coolest*. You have created this safe space (your art-mosphere), and you are its keeper. This should make you feel the most comfortable!

Because of your previous hard work and commitment, you get to experience first day excitement, steadiness, and hope, instead of first day unknown jitters! This magic was born from your heart and soul, and all of the people gathering to watch or collaborate with you want to be a part of your magic. And as Elizabeth Gilbert would say, "this is some BIG MAGIC!"

If you have made the room, you are qualified to be there. You are qualified to take up space and use your voice. You're qualified to lead and share in it. You are *beyond* qualified actually. You're a star shooting into the night, lighting up the sky. You've created hope, possibility, and places for art to be made and ideas to be shared. You are fully capable of dreaming your dream because you're already doing it.

UNDER PRESSURE

At many points throughout this book I might sound like the queen of butterflies and rainbows, but I'm able to be that way because I know how to sift through (and sit in) the bad stuff. With the good, there's always a mirror of challenges. When you've expanded, and you suddenly realize that the film you originally thought was going to be made up of nine people now needs to be thirty, that stuff jolts you. It becomes a scary step within a mountain of previously made scary steps that makes you wonder: *do I actually have the ability to get this done on a deadline and a super tight budget?*

There are times where we find ourselves *deeply* under pressure. (Cue the 80's song. I seriously love that thing.) Now comes the time where I really want to write the correct words, because as your creative partner and friend here, I know how you feel. I'm going to ask you to practice two things: gratitude, and recognizing what's rational versus irrational pressure.

Whenever I am met with pressure, I remind myself of these two unbelievably powerful concepts. One, being gratitude.

If I face the heat that's flashing in the pan and it attempts to come up to bite me, I try to replace the outlook with gratitude. I know it sounds crazy, but I promise, reverse psychology totally works. Thank you for challenging me. Thank you for forcing me to expand. Thank you for making me question my intentions. Thank you for making me work harder. Thank you for making me work quicker. Thank you for making me aware of never wanting to collaborate with that person again. You see? It takes the bite out of it.

The second concept that really helped me is to acknowledge whether this is actual pressure coming from somewhere else, or it's something that's come from inside my crazy brain. Am I projecting onto my situation, and therefore wasting my energy worrying? Or am I creating all of these barriers for myself out of fear, and poking myself in my own cage without any tigers there? I know it's really hard to accept, but eight times out of ten, if you're feeling pressure when it comes to your own creative entity, you are putting it on yourself. And that's freeing, right? Because we can reflect, we can renew, and we can start again.

I first learned the concept of 'renew' from my sophomore acting teacher, K. Jenny Jones. It was a big one for me. I later continued this decoding, renewing, and unwiring/rewiring magic with my therapist, who I'll later talk about in Chapter 10, Keeping Up With #1.

When we step back to take a moment, reflect, and then ask ourselves to consider gratitude and rationalize pressures, it defuses our internal ticking time bomb. As we know, life happens, so it's up to us to be aware of our triggers and be ready for those curve balls, because when you're in production or presentation mode, those curve balls are a comin'!

ANTICIPATE IT

Another incredible thing my therapist does with me as we rewire or face a scary thing is to anticipate the pressures, or plan what we're going to do in advance when everything hits the fan. And the coolest thing is, when we do this, seventy percent of the time it doesn't happen! But I've anticipated it, thought it through, and already met with it, so that when most of the really challenging things come my way I don't fumble as much in the moment. There will always be curve balls, but we can keep ourselves more agile and in-the-game if we anticipate it.

Every single time I begin something new, I allow my backlogs of history and experience to inform the creative process ahead. But this is always going to be different because the content or some of the people involved will be different. Every experience is unique. Remember in Chapter 6 when we talked about positive repetition when it comes to building with our teammates? Well, there can be red flag repetitions as well. When we notice one, we have to be sure to take note of it, because the next time we meet that red flag in our creative process or collaborations, we want to be able to take a deep breath (literally) and navigate it better this time.

When we clock those red flags and take them with us, they become a part of our arsenal. I would like to think makes us even more aware as creative leaders.

Anticipate the pressures, anticipate your potential recurring challenges, and anticipate that good ol' imposter syndrome will stop by once or twice. Welcome them, and then show them out your front door and send them on their un-merry way.

IMPOSTER BUSTERS

I just came up with this title, so I hope you can indulge me in yet another 80's tune and join me in singing, "who ya gonna call... IMPOSTER BUSTERS!" (Forgive me that the lyric doesn't quite fit within the meter). I hope that by now in this journey I can reveal a bit more about myself: I have a deep obsession with anything commercial that can also be celebrated loudly during *Halloween-town*, I mean, Halloween time. What can I say, it keeps me inspired!

So, when all these evil voices show up in your head, who ya gonna call? *You ain't afraid of no ghost,* and you're gonna to seek one of your favorite "imposter busters"—a dear friend, a member of your creative tribe, or a family member who you trust and who believes in you and your crazy ideas. I promise that you at least have one of these people in your circle, and if you need an extra, our team is always here for you.

The OG imposter buster in my life was my loving father. When I was young, he would always take his time to remind me it was okay that I might be a bit different than other kids or teens, and that there was nothing wrong with me for having really big dreams that we all knew would take me out of the great state of Kentucky. I cherished the heart-to-hearts we would have in our cozy family room/basement as a teenager, and he would always take the time to ask me, "How are you *really* doing?"

My dad supported my dreams as easy as it was for him to breathe. He would always look at me with such wonder, and he was always so proud of how zany my thoughts were, or how I might approach my creativity. The more outside the box I thought, the more things were supported by my dad. He always cheered me on. That cheering section was expanded by my other family members after his passing. I have always been extremely lucky to come from a family who believes in my dreams and the bigger picture I've always imagined and thrown myself at.

Other than my immediate family, my partner, and my therapist, my favorite imposter buster is my dear friend and fellow producer, Mitchell Walker. Ever since we met in the glorious dorms of Cincinnati College-Conservatory of Music, he has always supported and believed in me. No dream has ever been too big to discuss with Mitchell, whether it was planning our first summer stock season together getting to play a bunch of our dream roles, expanding my production company once we moved to the big city, or now, by making an album together that ended up hitting the Billboard's Top 10 charts during a pandemic.

Mitchell is the kind of friend who has always taken the time to listen to me, who has always made time to connect with me, and who has always been open with me. He's the kind of friend who will always joyfully bounce ideas off of (and with) me, and above all, has been one of the safe spaces for my creativity as a young mind in this industry. It's hard in these streets y'all, so we have to find ourselves some people that we can approach as our confidants. Now, just like when we're expanding our team, these people don't show their faces overnight. Sometimes they don't even show their faces for years. You just have to see that they're a safe place through their actions over long periods of time.

Mitchell is one of the most consistent and loving teammates I've ever had. And this doesn't mean we speak all day every single day, but in some seasons we do. I know he is always there for me not only personally, but also creatively as a sounding board. At the end of the day, I know he will try to encourage me, especially if I'm wondering whether or not I should take additional action on something new. Mitchell was actually the first person to know I was going to journey into expanding #BYOP and write this book. And you better believe he was proud of me, excited for me, and cheered me on.

Other Imposter Busters that I couldn't have done without in my life and early parts of my career include my hero and hometown musical theatre teacher at Dancensation Studios, Sandra Rivera, and her partner in crime, Mr. Frank Goodloe; my best friend from Kentucky's Governor's School for the Arts, Ben Ochsner aka "Benny Boo"; my loving teachers from Cincinnati College-Conservatory of Music, especially the inspiring Richard Hess, and the electric Patti James; the kind, pioneer leader, D. Lynn Meyers of the Ensemble Theatre of Cincinnati; and the resilient Aymie Majerski, my first female producing mentor in film.

IF IT SCARES YOU, JUST SAY YES

There have been a few times over my creative journey that have frightened the crap out of me. The most recent was when I was asked to do a one-woman show by one of my favorite directors and playwrights, A.S. Freeman. Now, this wasn't just any one-woman show about cleaning out your past loves with the dresses from your closet, it was a one-woman show where I would play all of the characters from Charles Dickens' timeless holiday classic, *A Christmas Carol*. This included my favorite guy, the loveable humbug himself, Scrooge.

Just seeing this in writing makes me laugh because it was such a ridiculous undertaking. It was very well written, and it was presented at the most darling theatre in a Hallmark picturesque town in Missouri. Alex (A.S.) called and asked me to do this role in October when it was scheduled to open at the beginning of December in 2018. I almost died. But what killed me even more was that I almost talked myself out of it several times because I was terrified.

I think a lot of creatives miss out on opportunities because we're scared. How many things have you said no to because you just didn't know where to begin? Here is what I want to share with you that changed everything: I asserted myself and acknowledged that I was scared, and I also asserted Alex. I told him on the phone that I could only succeed in doing this if he was supportive of me, both personally and creatively, as I attempted to take on this new role and responsibility. He kindly and brilliantly stated, "That's the only way I was planning on doing this."

I felt safe, I felt supported, and I felt cheered on. In that moment, Alex allowed me to be present and honest. And wouldn't you know, that's exactly what he wanted from me in my acting work, too. That right there gave me the courage to show up halfway across the country already partially off book, and allowed us to get the show up with just six rehearsals.

At the end of the day, I do have to give myself a little credit. Alex created an incredible environment for me, including equipping me with the most amazing stage management team, Kate and Jim. But I also showed up every day and screamed in the face of my fears. I worked through the anxiety, got on my feet, asserted it, and looked it in the eye until it eased just enough to let me do my show. If I'm being honest? The fear never completely went away. Every night, my assistant stage manager, Kate, would hug me backstage before I stepped out into the light. The fear would usually leave about seven minutes in, and then it felt exhilarating. I was driving my own car and I knew I had full control for everyone to see. I had said *yes*, and it was one of the biggest rewards I've received to complete the journey.

One of the main takeaways from this story is about learning to create a safe space for our creatives and teammates. My entire experience of this show was shaped with just one leader's awareness and kindness. Let's aim to be like this; let's be more like Alex.

SISTAS, WE FLY!

Now that we've decided we're only moving forward, taking those action steps one-by-one, we've officially alerted the masses. This is what tells the universe and the creative Gods that we're here to stay, and that we're not playing around. Some shiz is about to go DOWN! Sistas, we fly! Let's do this!

#BYOP

CHALLENGES FOR PART TWO:
INSPIRATION & IDEA

#BYOP CHALLENGE 6:
WHAT SERVES YOUR STORY?

1. Is there a story or project that you feel called to dive into and explore at this very moment? Let's write those ideas down. Let's make an idea arsenal to have as we explore this book and our creativity.

2. Which idea is jumping off the page to you? It might be the one that you've been wanting to strike the match on for a while now, or it could be that project that you've had planted as a seed in your heart but you haven't yet given yourself the time to move forward. It's the idea that creates energy! Circle it and move that idea to a new page or google doc sheet.

3. This chosen idea can be expressed in any art form or structure. There is no right or wrong way to go, but there will be a medium that probably suits your story better than the others. What option do you feel the most clearly aligns with this idea?

4. What medium do you feel best serves the story?

5. What medium and structure best serves the audience's experience of this story?

6. What medium do you feel might be the most accessible to you in the moment logistically or financially? Do you have friends or potential collaborators around you also hungry to dive in and explore this medium and story with you?

7. If it's new and unknown territory, even better! Let's just be sure to do our research up front and be ready to anticipate a longer timeline of learning.

8. Having gathered all of this information, has the medium become anymore clear?

#BYOP CHALLENGE 7: CAN I PICK YOUR BRAIN?

1. With this idea that we're now getting ready to step into and explore, who in your circle (or within your acquaintances) knows this medium or structure a little more confidently that you do?

2. We're going to reach out to them. People, especially artists, most likely won't mind sharing their past experiences with you in conversation.

3. Have you done as much research as you can so that you're able to have a somewhat educated conversation on this matter with another person who you mind consider to be more of an expert? If you haven't, you need to spend some time here to be the most efficient in the long run. Remember, the overall goal is to learn and become more self-sustaining!

4. Write down all of your questions so you know the exact information you're seeking. This makes it easy for when you need to pull up your questions as notes in a meeting or copy and paste them into an email.

5. Remember, you're still in the brainstorming phase, this is only to gather more intel!

#BYOP CHALLENGE 8:
TEAMING UP

1. After you've done your research and are starting to see where your holes might be as you move forward, write down the skill sets and personalities of positions that you don't feel confident in or haven't done personally.

2. Take inventory of your existing circle. Since this is a relationship-based business, is there any person in your direct circle who you feel might be able to help you with these missing holes in your business or be on your team?

3. Write down your values, how you wish to express your creativity, and how you expect to do business. What communication strategies are important to you? How often do you feel you'll need to lean on someone else? Looking back at your artist's recipe, how do you prefer to collaborate? I told you it would come in handy!

4. Write down the expectations of that position such as title, time commitment, amount of work needed, and what you can afford to pay or what perks you can offer them for joining your team.

5. Does this person in mind have the same values in business as you? Do they align with how you treat people? Do you feel they can be an appropriate extension of you if you are not around or on every email chain?

6. If the answer is no or this person cannot commit to your needs, ask for help within your circle for a recommendation.

7. If no one in your immediate circle is the right fit or they can't recommend a person who is, use the skills and information above to open your needed position to the public.

8. Take your time with interviewing and hiring. There's no rush, even when it feels like there is. We want to make sure you're welcoming the correct person onto your team and that they meet the criteria of everything important to you. Business Bombers Beware!

#BYOP CHALLENGE 9:
PRIORITIZING PRESSURES & PROCRASTINATION

1. Journal right now! Are these pressures you're feeling good or bad? If they're good pressures, like being too busy or having multiple job offers to consider, take a moment to be grateful. We need to be thankful for *all* good problems. They can be so rare to come by these days!

2. What on this list are the "no good, very bad" pressures? Are there any that you might be creating within your own private mind? If so, forgive yourself for not being a machine and take some time to reflect. You've gotten yourself so far already! This too shall pass. Walk it out, crank up the self-care, and talk these internal pressures out with your most trusted friend or confidant. When I get like this, I get my therapist on speed dial!

3. For the real pressures and problems like deadlines, bills, household issues, grief, or health scares, write them down. Now make time in your schedule FIRST to deal with the harder things that must be handled.

4. Once you knock out these real pressures and challenges, give yourself some time to process and begin the overall

journey. Whether it takes a day, or a weekend or even needs your focus for a whole month or year, you'll have much more energy to give to yourself and your creativity if you do this first. You'll also see very clearly what you have additional capacity for! You've got this!

#BYOP CHALLENGE 10: WHO YOU GONNA CALL? IMPOSTER BUSTERS!

1. I can guarantee that you're going to need a confidant (or five!) at this point to give you pep talks about expanding your creativity or small business, build you up over text, or ugly cry into a glass of wine with! Who are your personal and professional imposter busters?
2. Reach out to them and tell you how much you appreciate them with no strings attached.
3. Enjoy feeling all snuggly inside.

#BYOP

PART THREE

ACTION

8

LIGHTNING STRIKES

great idea holds zero power without action. Taking action is the most important ingredient of anything that we'll talk about in this book. Without taking action, we can never get what's in our head and imagination out for others to experience. It is imperative that we take action. We must honor our goals and dreams. Taking action is what creates energy. It is literally that energy that becomes your momentum in what moves the project forward. From starting a task list, to pre-production and post, it all comes down to taking action.

And sometimes when action is taken, lightning strikes. Energy is cultivated and begins to expand beyond our wildest dreams. A project dances out of the imagination and onto the page into a glorious combination of strength, storytelling, and outreach. It grows and flourishes. It rises and defies all expectation, and you know that you've helped cultivate something that is nothing short of divine creative intervention. And oh, how lucky, that *you* get to be one of its makers!

We must continue to move swiftly. We must listen more intently now than ever before, and become a part of our projects' ebb and flow. We must react, but with discernment; take our time, but remain steady. Now is the time to think even bigger than before.

THE BOLT

Every day, I wear a lightning bolt around my neck that was a gift from my dear friend, Michelle, of Michelle Fantaci Fine Jewelry, who I've known (and worked with) for well over six years. I told Michelle when she gave this necklace to me last Holiday season that I would never take it off. To this day, I still haven't. It keeps me going. It reminds me of the choice and power I have every single day to be the bolt that makes my dreams come true. I'm able to be a bolt of lightning for myself and others because I have the ability to *choose* to take action. I have the ability to claim my dreams, and I have the ability to make lightning strike! This bolt encourages me every day that if I keep stepping forward, there will be many moments where I get to sit at the precipice of the great creative vortex.

BIG MAGIC

I need to take a moment to give my deepest gratitude to the great Elizabeth Gilbert. Sometimes we have heroes within our own personal circles, and sometimes we have heroes where the only interaction we have with them is through their work. Reading her book,

Big Magic changed my life. I would not be writing my own book and wouldn't have launched my creative consulting lane without her book's encouragement. Reading her words forced me into even more action. As you can see through these pages, action for me has always been something I've taken, but I struggled with both my calling and personal value for a bit. These two things were clear: I was taking action, but I didn't know *why* I was taking it. Elizabeth's book helped me to better assert my ideas, and her earlier memoir, *Eat Pray Love* helped me to do reflective exploration in my personal life. She helped me to unlock my own #BIGMAGIC.

Immediately after closing her book, I started to align like never before. I began to heal from certain pieces of my past, and I began to fuse. Every time I would assert my big magic in life or on a project, I would hashtag it. I swear, I must have tagged it over a thousand times now. My favorite thing to do was to announce this newly cultivated #BIGMAGIC. It was my way of publicly and creatively stating, *I'm onto something, so get ready to experience it.*

So, my friends, get ready to experience some *Big Magic.*

FRANKIE! THE MUSICAL

A few years ago, I met a young lady through the award-winning acting studio I teach at, A Class Act NY. I am deeply proud of the children who train with us there. We've had students who star on hundreds of TV shows like *Stranger Things* and *This is Us,* and I've personally had students who have starred as the young princesses in *Frozen* on Broadway, and Ti Moune, who starred in the most gorgeous revival of *Once on this Island,* and in Jordan Peele's movie, *Us.* Children are extraordinary, but especially when they are first starting to flourish in what will become a piece of their lifelong passion and expression. I love teaching. It brings me absolute joy!

One day, I was virtually set up with 14-year-old Elise Marra from Michigan. Elise was really sweet, and was quite educated about the musical theatre cannon. She always wanted to work on multiple songs within an hour lesson. She reminded me a lot of myself at that age. You could tell she hadn't quite come into her own (I was also a late bloomer), but all I cared about—and what drove me to drive her—was her work ethic. We had that in common. We would train. We would work musical theatre pieces. We would collaborate. We would pass ideas back and forth with her other vocal coaches in Michigan to help her grow in her artistry. Elise would even accompany herself half of the time, so we'd also work that into becoming a part of her performance. She was always more confident and centered when singing behind the piano. The Marra's were loyal patrons of ACANY, so every time they came into the city, we also got to train in person. They also asked me to one of her music competitions in the upstairs space of Carnegie Hall. I remember feeling so proud to see Elise perform confidently that day.

Elise and I were online one night finishing a lesson (we expanded our sessions to two hours at times), and we had about ten minutes left when she asked if she could play me one last song—of course I said yes, expecting another tune from *Waitress*. I was already going through song titles in my head, when she said, all stealth like, "Cool beans, I'm going to play you one I wrote."

Now, at this point I knew this kid was driven and gifted, so I was aware of her potential, but I had absolutely no idea what was about to come out of this girl. I'll tell you right now what it was: it was her future.

Elise played and sang, and my body just started to tingle. I've had other kids and even friends show me their work before that

I was deeply proud of, but at the same time knew that it wasn't going to cause the musical theatre world to make way, shift, and open a space for them. And immediately, as Elise played a song from *Frankie! The Musical*, the beginning of her path began to carve out. When she finished, my jaw was on the floor. I couldn't believe what I'd just witnessed. It all made sense now—at least she did to me as an artist, anyway. This girl was not only meant to mix show tunes awkwardly through her braces, she was called to write them. She was called to compose them. She was called to forge a path for teens who write original works and musicals. She was called to create.

I had to think fast. There was so much potential, but so many constraints. First, Elise was in another state. Second, it's a boundary of the studio that we're not supposed to speak to our students outside of the classroom because of the overwhelming linkage of social media. I couldn't just begin a relationship outside of teaching Elise. I don't play that way. So, we had to keep the lessons going. I had Elise tell her mom that I would speak with them more in depth (and on the clock) when they visited me at the office of the studio in New York. I wanted to help her develop in other areas of her creativity, but we would have to do it in the last few minutes of her regular musical theatre classes.

So, we did. And we continued to do it under this structure for more than a year. I would give gentle feedback on her material at the end of her lessons, and I also started to lightly fill her family in, that surprise! I am also a producer. Elise kept writing, and there were now multiple musicals and a few plays. At this point, this girl was only 15! So, we kept moving.

Elise had recently done the Southeastern Summer Theatre Institute in 2018, and also connected deeply with one of the conference's directors, Joe Barros. Joe had assisted on New York shows like *Gigi* on Broadway, and was a brilliant out-of-the-box thinking guy. He also worked beautifully with kids, so Joe, on his end, also started to work with Elise on the book and music of *Frankie!* After collecting this information from Elise's incredible mom at the end of our lessons, I started to lay out a path of what we would do for Elise's musical in the real world. One day, after I connected with Joe, he and I decided we just had to do it. We had to take action. It was important. Elise had to be introduced to the world because she was going to change it! I told Miss Jessica, the owner of the studio, that one of Elise's projects was ready for real commercial development, and there was movement from multiple people to help her in this venture. Although she hadn't yet seen this side of Elise, she respected what we were doing and supported the project.

Joe and I went full steam into an industry reading of *Frankie! the Musical* in the summer of 2019. With the help of my ever-devoted casting director, Daryl Eisenberg, and her now partner, the incredible Ally Beans, we assembled a kick-butt cast, and also created interest for some others to be attached to the future of the piece. There is so much strategy involved in these choices, especially when you have a (now) 16-year-old composer. You have to get kind and good people into the room: people you would trust with a child's work and who would take it seriously. You have to get people who have enough clout to help draw attention to the piece and who bring their own energy to the room to help the piece expand. And Finally, you need to get people in the room who understand life enough to check their egos at the door and realize that sometimes it's fully appropriate to take direction from a teenager. We welcomed the darling, Autumn Hurlbert to the company, Broadway staple, Jason "SweetTooth" Williams, and budding starlet, Delphi Borich to the cast. The team respected Elise greatly, so we had to continue on with this trend. A large part of this process also became about building Elise's confidence and teaching her how to create and manage her own work. We also wanted her to understand how to take proper command of a room, how to work with a real music director, and also, how to be her own producer. Ring a bell?

The reading was packed, and that positive ball of energy just kept growing. Usually, the next step would be to do an out-of-town run or developmental production of the piece, but my gut told me that wouldn't be the best choice for this. I'd taken some red flags that I previously captured from my experience of working on *The Dodgers*, and I realized we didn't just want to spend money to have an additional production without a clear future for the piece. It would then just become a continual game of fundraising for the future.

One of Elise's many tasks was to begin social media for *Frankie!* as the piece started to expand, and make sure she was starting a relationship with fans. It was through listening to them and what they wanted that we found the answer to what the next move was: people wanted to hear the music. People wanted to hear, sing, and share the music, so we decided to continue our creative process unconventionally: we were going to make a cast concept album before the show had ever had an actual on-stage performance.

Creating a concept album was more affordable and immediate than other options, and therefore within our control. We knew this would give us additional products to push out as pitching material, and that it had endless accessibility to help raise awareness of our new show. This idea seemed like it would give us a true shot to create longevity in introducing Elise to the playground of commercial musical theatre and the NYC market.

We began to build out from the sides again. We connected with Daryl and Ally to build out a smaller cast, and we were extremely lucky to connect with Tony nominee, Caitlin Kinnunen to sing the title role of Frankie. Whoever sang the role of Frankie needed to be someone who had carried a show before. They also needed to have the chops and experience to repeatedly sing lead vocals on ten songs over the course of two days. We didn't have a lot of time in the studio because of a tight budget, so each moment was planned precisely around about 30 people's schedule, and we had to *move*. And all of this was in motion not yet knowing that a world pandemic was looming around the corner.

Late fall 2019, when we knew we were positioning this album to be a real thing, I pitched my friend Van Dean about distributing the album through his label, Broadway Records. He quickly said yes, and I was floored. My friend Mitchell and producing partner on the album (who I previously mentioned as my favorite imposter buster) predicted that Broadway Records would cheerfully agree to take on the album. Of course, they did, so he had the right to brag about telling the future. Another cool fact is that Van and I began producing around the same time in the early 2010's. We had sushi once, and he explained to me his idea of starting Broadway's future most prominent record label. And lo and behold, he did. Come up together, I tell you!

As we approached the studio with Broadway Records attached, we knew we were set up for success. Mitchell, who had now grown into being one of the most incredible record producers I have ever witnessed, conducted the symphony of *Frankie!* from the control booth. I kept my lead on further expansion, like making sure the great Michael Kushner was documenting everything for us visually for future press, and trying to get Elise an agent because I had a feeling future deals would be coming. We had invested, so now, we had to be protected. As a producer, it's your duty to think ten steps ahead to help create action steps.

Enter my amazing literary agent, Amy Wagner from A3 Artists Agency, who also encouraged me to write this book. Amy has been one of the biggest cheerleaders of my career thus far, and was hip to coming trends before every person in the industry saw it coming. Amy, with the encouragement of my acting agent Richard Fisher, has always pushed me to create in all of my lanes at once. She could see the benefits of how encouraging me to create kept me moving and well oiled. Also, as two smart business women, I knew if I worked with anyone who showed massive promise, I had a safe person to introduce them to. Above all things, I am loyal, and I wanted to introduce Elise to A3 in a glorious setting. A3, previously Abrams Artists Agency, had done so much for me. Now, instead of Amy experiencing Elise's work virtually from a bedroom in Michigan, she got to be introduced to Elise in a state-of-the-art studio in New York City, with a full team functioning around her while she made creative decisions in real time.

The album debuted on Friday, May 29th 2020. We decided to hold strong and release the album on this date even though a pandemic had recently set off like an atomic bomb. People were locked in their homes and needed some joy and levity, and what better to bring people hope than a musical written by a person who could barely drive a car? The night before the Friday release, my gut knew that in order to get this thing to launch loudly during a pandemic, I needed my friends in the industry to post about *Frankie!* And that was to become the only time to post about the album. Thursday night was also the beginning of the global protests over the murders of George Floyd, and Breonna Taylor, who was shot to death in my hometown of Louisville, Kentucky.

Because of these tragedies, it became the wrong time to boast and push *Frankie!* the way you normally would with an album's release. That Tuesday, our album stood proudly with Broadway Records and participated in the music industry blackout. We also went silent for a week on our social media. It was the only option for us. It's what we felt called to do and put the focus where it was needed the most—on actual issues in the world that needed our utmost attention.

During that opening weekend, a seed that would help us to create further longevity for *Frankie! The Musical* was planted in the face of what our world had become: a pandemic and a revolution. *Frankie! The Musical's* cast concept album became the #1 musical theatre album on iTunes, passing *Hamilton* at 1:00pm on its release day. I feel like Lin Manual Miranda would give Elise big 'ups' for this. The album became the 5th best-selling soundtrack that weekend, debuted at #9 on Billboard's Soundtrack Chart, and held there for two weeks! Pretty nifty, if I do say so myself. I am a proud producer.

In the face of everything, we kept going. But when the industry needed us to stop, we stopped with it. We listened, used discernment, and then we proceeded. I'm happy to say *Frankie!* is still alive and well, and the property and Elise now both have a pretty stellar agent. I know this piece will continue to grow because of its message, team, and its creator, Elise. #THEFUTUREISFRANKIE

WORK BEGETS WORK

This is one of my favorite sayings of all time! Work begets work. And it's true! When you help create something really great and remain consistent with it, people will begin to take notice and come to you with additional work opportunities. Do you need something done? Give it to someone who identifies as a busy person.

The quickest way to achieve more lightning strikes is to get to work. I always say that in New York City, the quickest way to getting a job you want is by taking a job you don't want. Your actions inform the universe that you're down to do the hard work. Have you ever heard the saying "Opportunity usually shows up to your door looking a lot like work."? Another major truth: we have to pay our dues, and we have to do the work. There are no shortcuts in life, and the work that might seem easiest is usually just a detour to nowhere.

When we work, we become the artists who continually generate consistent outputs of energy. We become known for this. We need many pieces to fuel our ideal dream work. We need finances, connections, relationships, ideas, and teams, but all of these things can all be found from working hard and working anywhere, especially when you live in New York or LA.

BOY HERO

Sometimes lightning strikes by way of positive motion, and sometimes lightning strikes by way of tragedy. Do you remember in Chapter 4, "Starting From Scratch," I mentioned how sometimes inspiration can be planted as a seed? I wanted to plant that idea for you back then so we could discuss it now.

One of the projects dearest to my heart is my original screenplay, *Boy Hero*. It was inspired by the comic book trial of 1954, and a panel I saw at Comic Con in New York City. The experience of receiving the original inspiration was by far the most vivid of any of my creative ideas.

In 2014, I was given a press pass for Comic Con after finishing a modeling gig. When I stepped inside, the ground floor of the Javits Center was bustling with superheroes and comic book characters. I felt like I was at an indoor, air-conditioned Disney World! It was all so curious to me! I had never been to Comic Con before, and I was blown away by the interaction and engagements happening with fans. I come from the world of Broadway, and I thought we had the most enthusiastic fans, but this was on another level!

I went downstairs to check out the smaller panels, which were much more my style as a newbie, and headed into *The Time American Librarians Saved Comic Books.* Now, I don't know about you, but the library was one of my favorite places in the world when I was growing up. I would always find a reason to sneak up to the empty library in my childhood church, or the glorious, renovated, state-of-the-art library in my hometown of Jeffersonville, in Louisville. Throw in being a 90's kid and seeing movies like *The Pagemaster,* and I was a library fan for life! I've always loved reading. I haven't always had the discipline to do it, but I love libraries and librarians. I always looked to them for knowledge, and I remember them as being extremely kind to me because I was a curious kid.

I went into this panel, and a lovely woman by the name of Carol Tilley commanded the space, telling us the story of "the great comic book trial". I listened to her talk, completely dumbfounded. There was a trial on comic books? Like, for real?! She started naming the real-life 'characters' who played a major role in the story such as Frederic Wertham, a children's psychiatrist who thought comic books were the culprit of juvenile delinquency in the 1950's. I sat there taking in this information while my brain was going into overdrive. As Carol spoke, I visualized librarians meeting with children and forming secret book clubs after school across the US. The children she spoke about wrote 217 letters to the US Senate to save comic books, so I envisioned these teachers and librarians working with the kids, and sharing the importance of fighting to be able to continue to read them. Then, a very quiet and gentle idea was placed in my heart. What if we theatricalized this moment? What if instead of 217 letters being written to the Senate, we see the children actually *going* to the Senate, led by one librarian, to save comics?

Keep in mind that in 2014, I hadn't written anything before. I had no idea how to even begin. I'd wanted to write a screenplay before, and had even written an outline for a story very close to me, but to write a full screenplay? Absolutely not. I thought at the time, *who am I to even want to begin to take on that venture?* But I also knew deep within my soul that this was my story to tell. So, this idea was planted until I was ready to take action on it. I knew what had happened in history on that powerful day in April of 1954, but I needed my reason to tell this story. I needed to live some more and keep my eyes open.

Some nudges began to happen. Elizabeth Gilbert's *Big Magic*, for one. She told a story about how she had begun to write a novel once, and let time pass to where she wasn't actively working on it, and lo and behold, that exact story ended up coming out of her dear friend. That was my baby nudge.

A bigger nudge was that screenplay outline I mentioned above—a film I'd already begun working on that was inspired by a personal event from my life. I was determined to see that project through, and it was in deep development over that next year. Unfortunately, some red flags were beginning to pop up over that challenging experience. I was working with a team who, on paper, knew how to make a full-length feature film, but every fiber of my being told me from what I was observing to protect my comic book idea. It wasn't the right time for it to come out of me.

That is, until the fall of 2016. My father and my hero, the great, kind, loving, and talented, Ernie Adams, left this earth on August 20th, 2016. He passed after a wicked five week known battle with cancer. We found out the news after he was having severe stomach pains, and was immediately moved to the cancer wing at a local hospital in Kentucky.

It was the greatest tragedy of all of our lives. My dad was a larger than life guy with a spirit that permeated every space he was ever in. He was everyone's favorite guy, and everyone's go-to person to share a joke or have a connected personal moment with. He was also known around town for his unearthly bass singing voice, and for his love of his beautiful wife, Dana, and three children, Ashley Kate, Wesley Chace and Audrey Belle. I am so lucky that I got to make him a father.

My dad was a rock to many people. To give you an idea of impact, we are a family of mainly musical theatre performers and musicians. We have no true status in the Kentucky elite, but there were over 750 people present for his funeral. The lines were wrapped down the hall, and around the outside of the building for his funeral home visitation. This is because my father was a father to so many. But he was *my dad*. He was my closest rock and confidant. I am blessed that I got to be nurtured by him for as long as I did.

So, staring at a blank computer screen while sitting on my parent's back porch as my Uncle Wayne and Mom were going through paperwork about financials, my gut and heart decided it was time to take action on my first screenplay. I had lost everything in my personal world, so what was left to lose? Absolutely nothing. And I thought, *wouldn't this be a great story if I could actually complete this?*

I revisited my old inspiration of the comic book trial, which I had kept warm in my heart, and I began to write. I didn't exactly know how to start, so I began with the things that I knew I understood: the characters and dialogue.

I do believe that writing helped me to heal. I've always said when I can't do anything else, I write. And how true is this statement as I'm writing each word of this book to you today during the great pandemic of 2020. Many other projects had to pause, but I'm still writing. I would light a candle each time I wrote, and invite my father to come sit with me. *Boy Hero* is an inspirational, family-friendly feature film that follows a revolutionary librarian as she teaches a non-verbal student to read by using comic books. They band together to uphold the freedom of reading by marching to the New York State Senate together to save comics. I sat down for an hour almost every day over the course of the next year to write the first draft of my original feature screenplay. My dad continued to support this venture with his energy, but this time in a completely different way.

I processed my life while I was writing this screenplay. Each character in the story experiences my family's most personal navigation of grief—seeing a world with completely new eyes, feeling the warmth of my dad's love as a blanket over this story, and celebrating a young lady who will do everything in her power to make sure all stories are able to be told in the face of adversity.

CONDUCT ELECTRICITY

As an artist, we hold the power to conduct our own electricity. We know what lives inside us, and we're the only ones who are aware of what must come out. I encourage you to conduct your own electricity in the face of all positive and tragic seasons of your life.

Continue to tell your stories in the face of adversity because like your goals, they are the most sacred parts of you. They are the most authentic. And when you're experiencing your most beautiful and harrowing moments, you are the most connected to this thing called life. Your tragedy, pain, and love are universal, and your life experience has the ability to shape into your most powerful stories.

Grab your lightning bolt and hold it high for all to see. Claim your power, your pain, and your stories, and move through them with action. They will carry you.

9

YOUR WORK IS YOUR WORK

I f you're anything like me, above all, you wish for this creative life to be able to function in perfect harmony, peace, and communion. We are *artists*. We wish for things to go smoothly. But the truth is, we are imperfect artists, and imperfect beings, and at times our art (and functioning with other artists) can be a reflection of this.

Sometimes collaborations won't go as planned, so we must learn to claim our work from the beginning. It's important to do this in every step of the creative process as the project expands. I know it might feel weird at times, and we don't want to come across as this ego-centered, power-hungry maniac, but we must proudly claim what is ours. We must claim our contributions without shame, and without hindrance. We need to state it and celebrate it. Your work is your work.

CREATED BY

Just because something isn't tangible yet doesn't mean you can't claim it. You can copyright outlines with the US Government, and you can time stamp ideas via email or by sending your outline through the mail. You can write up an NDA or deal memo if you have an idea, before you go to another person to collaborate.

I wish someone at the beginning of my content creating career would have told me that "created by" was even a thing. It is, and it's the most important thing! The amount of times I've created a concept, shared a fully formulated idea, and collaborated with another person who then business bombed me like a pro is a challenging amount. It pains me to look back at it. But, now that I've been kicked in the teeth, I have learned, and I'm here to do my best to make sure this never happens to you.

Always feel proud to put your name on your work. If you developed an idea, cultivated it, navigated it, created action steps for it and then went to a writer to help you further formulate it, you also OWN THAT WORK. That idea, timeline, story, series of events, and content was created by you. You should feel inclined to share credit with them, but in no way, shape, or form should you ever be excluded from this formula. If you are the flint in which helps to create the flame, you get to be a part of the fire.

To the people who have done this to me and to others: shame on you. But for you, my creative friend, we're going to continue to talk about ways to protect your art, so you can create freely and confidently.

PROTECTING YOUR HE(ART)

I love living in New York City. You feel the energy and rhythm of the city each and every single day just by being here. You can feel its heartbeat—a renewable power source that you can always tap into. I believe that NYC is the most resilient city. I believe it's always held the power of reinvention, and is the birthplace of inno-vation, structure, and world commerce. To me, it is the center of the world. I have found my joy and creative freedom here and I'm deeply in love with it.

A few years ago, a trend began to pop up on the sidewalks of Manhattan. Spray painted in neon blues and pinks was the warning to "Protect Your He(art)". As artists, we sometimes find these pieces of concrete in what feels like the most poetic of times. I needed this statement and reminder. It would always give me strength as I stepped into an audition or a meeting, and it always checked me. Did I have everything in order? Did I know how to present the right amount of information as I stepped forward with my creative ideas in sharing them with others? Was I protected?

I want to encourage you to take some simple steps to make sure there is another person who always has your best interest at heart. When you pass around your pitch or creative idea, there are simple ways you can protect the sharing of your idea.

1. Non-Disclosure Agreement (NDA). This is a docu-ment that acknowledges and protects information shared between two parties. Therefore, if you share your screen-play or podcast pitch with someone, you can ask them to sign an NDA to acknowledge that they have experienced taking in your creative idea and information and they can't share it with anyone else without your acknowledgement or permission.

2. Register your script with the Writer's Guild of America. This is inexpensive to do, and once complete can be plopped on the front of your script.

3. Copyright your script through the US Government.

4. Use the copy or CC function on your emails. Copy a trusted colleague, intern, or close friend when content is circulating. When we make new introductions or pitch our creativity to someone new, it's great to assert that someone else is aware of and copied into the conversation. And when called for, have no fear of the using the BCC function.

5. Assert your team and business. If you are signed with an agency, make sure that your materials acknowledge this. Your screenplay or novel outline should have your registered business on the front of it, especially if you are pitching it blindly.

6. Put your contact information and team members' bios into your pitch documents. This asserts your team, and what you all have built together. It's also part of the paper trail that links you to your own work. In a meeting, it's a transparent way to claim all people and roles involved or that may have been previously taken.

7. An MOU (Memorandum of Understanding). This is a new one that I have recently become acquainted with. It's a fabulous way to write down collaborators intentions as you start to collaborate with your intellectual property (IP) and time.

FREE-STANCE

As artists, we are predominantly functioning as freelancers. My friends, there is the utmost power in this! You can remain flexible, protect yourself, and create multiple lanes of income at the same time. Claiming this free-stance can allow you to have end-less amounts of opportunities, and much more freedom than the 9-to-5er.

There are pros and cons to this chosen world. Many of us art-ists are experiencing one of these thorns right now as we strug-gle to have our businesses recognized by the government so we can receive unemployment. This is why it's so important to claim our business legally, as I mentioned in Chapter 5 in the "Business Savvy" section. We need to have a paper trail and to keep those books for the worst-case scenario.

But to me, there is a much more limitless potential in our way of working if we claim free-stance. Freelancing is hard because it holds you accountable every single day. There are times when we don't know where our paychecks will be coming from two months from now. But when those opportunities begin to align with our tal-ents and we learn how to claim a side hustle that pairs well with our art, it becomes one of the *best* feelings. You can then truly become your own independent artist, agent, and creator. You can do what-ever you want, when you want, and things happening in the outer world will dictate your personal success, less and less.

We discuss creative strategies to claim all of our artistry, how to cultivate it for ourselves, and how to assert creative stability in the Multi-Hype workshop I created with Michael Kushner and Kimberly Faye Greenberg. In this workshop, we encourage other multi-hyphenates to navigate and claim their artistry and talk about how personal gifts can best serve you by creating longevity in a creative career. You can stay informed of all of our upcoming offer-ings at multihypeworkshop.com.

Claiming free-stance is hard. Being your own producer is hard. Creating your own work is hard, but is the most infinite venture. If you claim your free-stance from the vantage point of claiming your hard work, endless ideas, and opportunities, you will succeed.

GO WITH GRACE

On this journey, there will be creative projects that lose steam no matter how hard we work or how hard we try to convince others to work. One day it will just slowly begin to become stagnant, or your place in it may begin to feel unwelcome. You'll probably realize in reflection that this project is starting to take a lot of your joy away, exhausting you beyond belief, and causing you to start questioning many things for long periods of time. Some projects will have maybe made it to Chapter 4 or 6, and fallen off with a misstep of the chosen creative team. It's honestly the worst feeling when this happens, but for all of these projects we must let them go with grace, celebrate all of the moments of good and success within the journey, and collect all of those red flags to inform our later successes. We must give ourselves permission to continue to create somewhere else.

Like in any relationship, if you are not valued, you need to move on. This includes projects or creative ideas you have developed and given your life to for years, especially if it's affecting your quality of life. No project is worth your peace of mind. I'm going to say that again. *No project is worth your peace of mind.* It might feel like it's worth fighting for because so much of your identity has been wrapped up in this project until this point, but I promise you, if you let the dead weight go, the most glorious collaborations will come. We must take action and say no, and we must move on.

I have a hard story for you, but I'm going to tell it. It's why we're here. About six years ago, I received a call on a rainy Friday evening from a friend in London. He wanted me to take a look at this play he'd been helping to develop. It was a wonderful "New American Play" (as we later branded it), and it had the most potential of anything I had ever had the honor of reading. The potential was dripping off its pages through the fascinating and honest characters that told the story, and the setting was something completely original that hadn't really been done before in a play format. Additionally, the subject matter seemed oddly present at the time; it was timeless, and would continue to be more electric even now.

When I began this journey, I was a work for hire producer. I was paid a very small amount to produce the next steps of the play, show what I felt those steps might be, and present them to the team. We decided as a team to take action and to mount an industry reading in New York City. I used what I had at the time, which were my relationships, and reached out to friends I'd met personally or professionally in the industry, pitching them the show to gauge their interest, and letting them know an offer would be forthcoming.

At the first reading, we could tell we had a hit on our hands. My acquaintance, Finn Wittrock, kindly flew out from Los Angeles pre-Emmy nomination to lead this play for me. He was stellar. Collaborating with him, we brought on another incredible actor, movie star and now Disney prince, Billy Magnussen. My goal was to get some of the most authentic personalities and voices I'd ever met up on that stage together, and see them interact with this text. Billy, who once forced me into a dance contest at a ping-pong club, spotlight and all, was definitely authentic and charming.

The buzz was as buzzin' as you hope it to be, and as a young and budding producer I was getting introduced to people left and right. One person I was introduced to that day was my now collaborator and dear friend, Jim Kierstead, who would later become a big piece to the puzzle. While everyone was celebrating in the lobby, a vivacious investor from LA approached my general manager Evan and I, and the next step became clear. We were going to take this play to premiere on the west coast.

That day, we got our first investment into the next big steps, and since we'd already received a wave of momentum and support, we knew we had to follow it wherever it led. I asked for feedback from all seventy-five industry attendees, and we heard back from about twenty with really great information and notes that we planned to input where we felt appropriate. When in development, you have to consider your audience's opinion because they become the future ticket buyers, but you also need to hold strong to the piece's bottom line. This is art, and these are just a few of the thousands of puzzle pieces in the art of producing.

LA was an incredible choice for this show. Though it was challenging to both navigate a new town while in development *and* build a new show with a full set, it allowed the piece to grow, and we got to attach another group of loving actors and dear friends to it. Our west coast cast included Eric Nelsen, who I mentioned earlier, and Emma Hunton, one of my lifelong friends and co-star from *Gay Bride*. We were also lucky to have Corbin Bleu join the cast, too! We opened with a *bang!* There was a powerful energy flowing around this play that pushed the potential even further. But as the run continued and everyone began to go deeper, an underlying sense of subtle, growing separation began to surface as well.

When you're young and budding in your creative career, sometimes people don't believe in your methods, what you have to say, or how you go about saying it. They simply don't believe in your ability to lead because you don't have a big enough track record for them to trust you yet. Understand that in a way, we want people to volley with us—we want them to question and challenge us *to a point*... but sometimes, the depth of this volleying and challenging is a representation of a much larger issue or problem that has nothing to do with you. Creatives also take comfort in different things, but at this point in my career, I just didn't know that yet.

Unfortunately, in our business, these people do exist. Just imagine what happens when those people have to actually navigate major decisions with you. It becomes a nearly impossible challenge. It becomes difficult to function and be heard, to simply continue your work and do your job (which is to lead the project and encourage forward motion in the first place). It was my job to be this incredible show's cheerleader, and as I showed up day after day cheering it on, giving it my all consistently, in return, I was getting nothing but garbage spewed back at me. Every. Single. Day. And every day, I chose to prevail through the garbage because that's what I do. I don't give up. I don't give up on people, and I don't give up on projects.

Sometimes people will flat out be mean to you. I'm not talking about rolling their eyes when you're presenting or shooting you down in conversation, I'm talking straight up harassment and sending rude emails that belittle you and call you names. As many of you have also experienced, it's mind blowing sometimes how we can continue to face these things every single day for the sake of a project. When we find ourselves in these positions, we're usually in way too deep. We don't know what to do or how to keep claiming our years of hard work. We don't want to walk away, because then where does our artistic work go?! Is it negated? Does it just dissolve? Do we even get credit? Will people think we couldn't do it? My friends and creatives, it doesn't matter what they will think; we must let it go and walk away with grace.

We are not called to be placeholders. Your work is your work. Remember, if you built the room it is yours. I gave everything I had to build this show, but I was being horribly disrespected, and I had to appropriately hit the eject button. No one gets to behave like this. And the longer you stay in these types of creative situations, the longer you're showing the universe that you accept and will tolerate this behavior.

On top of the routine sludge that literally just became my work life (that I was choosing, by the way, because I created the LLC), I was being used as a placeholder. In this situation, as the lead producer, I was supposed to develop the piece, grow the piece, attach my relationships to the piece, shine it up, pitch it, position it, fundraise it.... and then just expected to hand it off.

Remember my dear friend Jim, who I previously mentioned? Jim is an accomplished Tony Award-winning producer. I was honored when he decided to attach himself to this piece right before we left for L.A. Jim has worked on several large Broadway properties from development, up. This was not his first rodeo by any means, and Jim deeply believed in how I was moving forward with the show. He appreciated that I led kindly, and he also appreciated how Evan and I managed to keep the budget down. Jim invested in us and believed in the magic we were making, and to some members of the creative team, he was much more ideal to lead this project than I was—much more. Jim is one of my mentors, so of course I agreed, and I attempted to share the option with him and become partners. But because I was budding, I was told that no one would trust me with their money. So, I tried to find a balance to protect the work I'd already accomplished in addition to my future work, and brought on someone with more experience to help me lead, but that was never approved or supported by the full team. If I was expected to drive the car, to make it my #1 priority every morning when I woke up, I still needed insurance. There comes a point when you have given something your all, and that just *has* to be enough.

It was time to move on, no matter how painful it was to let go. But I did it gracefully, while facing two of the hardest losses of my life. I took those red flags, stuffed them away in my heart, and something else really cool began to happen. All of the people who I loved working with (about 90% of our now large team), I continued to work with! And can you believe that other people had the same secret feeling that I was holding inside to appear and remain professional? We moved on to make things in easier environments, in a more fully supported fashion, joyfully. Good will still flow from the challenges if we have the courage to let go of the pieces that aren't vibing with our personal paths. Your work doesn't just disappear because the *right* people are already very aware of your capabilities.

So, dear reader of this book, there is no amount of tomfoolery you should accept, even if you are on the verge of the latest and greatest idea. If it steals away from the core of you, it's not worth it. I promise that resolve will come, healing will come, and hey, maybe one day you can share your own stories in a book just like this. It's okay to kindly let go of what is no longer serving you.

I'll leave this story with something I'm proud of: I never once disrespected the main energy that didn't agree with mine on this property. I remained kind to them in the face of all adversity, and continued on despite their harsh words because that's not how I roll. I wanted to be able to be proud of my actions, no matter the cost. We have to remain gentle with people, even when they are unkind within our own boundaries. We want to be able to sleep at night. We also don't know what these people are dealing with that might be encouraging them to act this way towards us. We still have to give them respect, but we also must keep our own. We must show them grace to go with grace.

PIVOTING UNLOCKS POWER

Just experiment. When we pivot our artistic output or open ourselves to other ideas, we will *thrive*. It's the whole "if you leap, a net will appear" thing. Pivoting during a huge life or world event is so important because making this brave choice can create longevity. When you show the universe that you're ready to dance, it'll become the best partner you've ever had.

At the beginning of the pandemic, I read in my morning news scroll that the businesses who'll survive are the ones that adapt and shift to be able to work during this time. It lit a fire under my tail to make sure I was able to get this book out of me in this season. It also informed the next action steps of my work—it informed me to pivot.

Most creatives who read this book are in this "creativity thing" for the long haul. We're here because we want a lifetime in the arts. In this lifetime, we'll have struggles, ups, and downs, but it's those struggles that help us to remain present. They are what keeps us on our toes, and they are what keeps both us and our art LIVING.

Welcome your need to pivot with gratitude and curiosity that will help inform the next steps of your expansion. Try to remain open in a closed world. It'll feel like an oxymoron, but I encourage you to try and do it anyway. Pivot. Enjoy the flexibility of the strategy, and allow it to inform new dreams. Pivoting unlocks power. It's what allows us to continue on with our work and creativity, no matter what adversity we might face outside of us.

10

KEEPING UP (TAKING CARE OF #1)

I feel like the time has come to check in. How are you doing? I know this is A LOT of information, and at times it can take a moment (or a season) to process. Sometimes when we challenge our creativity, it feels as though we're breaking down our previous belief systems, like we might do in therapy for our personal lives. Challenging our rewiring takes massive amounts of effort. Growing is completely necessary, but it's also exhausting. To get quiet with ourselves, release the shame, and allow ourselves to throw out this imaginary rulebook we created somewhere along the journey takes a lot of adaptive energy. Your history is beautiful, and where you're heading after all this new found energy and reflection is going to be super cool. I hope you're finding so much joy in this, and freeing yourself to step into all of the possibilities you truly have.

Along with the exciting progress and collaborations from our creativity, there comes a needed second helping of self-care. When you are outputting so much energy, consistently each and every day, you must take time to take care of yourself. You aren't seeking anymore, you're cultivating and being your own well, as my email from "The Universe" stated to me this morning. (You can get emails sent to you from "The Universe". How cute is that?)

My personal journey of learning to take care of myself is something that I've discovered gives me profound joy. I think it's because I didn't always know how to for the longest time, and in general, when most of us were children, it's not something that was really taught to us the same way we were taught to "say no to drugs", or to write out checks in 4H class. Self-care wasn't a fad, and merchandising hadn't yet allowed it to explode and become a forefront of our culture. In today's world, we have a better understanding of both self-care and taking care of our mental health. Personally, I cherish this type of inner reflection.

As a child, I often felt in almost every environment I was in that we never got too deep. I would have deep conversations about my aspirations, but in general, I wasn't sitting around having conversations with anyone about early life experience, trauma, or emotions. The first time I remember asking a critical thinking question was in my seventh grade Sunday school class. The question was about being genuine and how that might affect asking for forgiveness. I could immediately tell I was going to be a fish out of water.

Things "were as they were", and I never really saw many people question it.

We are artists. We experience things louder, and we need to learn to care for the vessels in which these emotions and experiences live in. I don't know about you, but I personally felt like Inspector Gadget for most of my childhood and adolescence. While most things in the south just weren't talked about, I was always asking questions, dissecting things in my head, and trying to make sense of everything around me, including dynamics and relationships. I was always so inquisitive. Like every Disney Princess imaginable, I wanted "adventure in the great wide somewhere", but I think what I was truly searching for was peace within myself and a large amount of understanding.

I wanted to be able to unlock what was inside and understand why I functioned the way I did, or why others may behave a certain way. I wanted to be able to speak the truth about my history, and learn to love and value myself.

My journey of learning how to take care of myself hasn't always been the easiest. It's been long, grueling, and I'm still actively learning how to do it. It's a never-ending journey. What I *can* tell you is that ever since I began that journey in my early 20's, my personal bottom line is now extremely different than it was back then. I now have alerts and guards that go off inside when I should be doing something else, or when I should take up more space or speak up. I'm also now more aware as to what I can do to fill my cup back up.

There are many ways we can rewire ourselves, but it does take time. If there's something that has been nagging at your heart—help that you want to get, support that you deserve—I want to encourage you to take it. For me, getting a therapist was one of the best choices I ever made in my life. It gave me the ability to make peace, and allowed me to grieve, flourish, and then grieve and flourish again with life, both presently and bravely. It's the best gift I have ever given myself.

I want to encourage everyone to take care of their mental health. When we do, we are the most loving, the most flexible, and the most open versions of ourselves. In my experience, when I take care of my mental health, I'm more ready to get down to business and jump wildly into my creative life.

FILL UP YOUR CUP

People are like cars, with our own little gas tanks. Sometimes we like to push ourselves to the limit and end up driving on fumes. Raise your hand if you're the type to drive around on the last gallon of gas for a little too long? (Don't worry, I just raised my hand, too). As I'm sure you've noticed once or twice, we have the tendency to do this personally as well.

We live in a culture that glorifies 'busy', and it makes it worse that we also all have little computers attached to our hands. We're always accessible even in life's most challenging moments; the boundaries are forever changing because of world events and technology.

I want to know (and I want you to know) what fills up your cup? Is it a night at home with your phone put away? Is it a nice long walk around your neighborhood? Do you enjoy yoga or bike riding? Do you love to read? What do you like to do that helps revive you? Do you fill up your cup alone, or with others?

Knowing what the smaller things are and how we can access them will make a great impact on our larger well-being and self-care. It's important to know, especially in times of crisis, what might make us feel better or bring us solace, joy, and peace.

For me, as I shared with you earlier in this book, my creativity is linked to my spirit, my person, and my body, so when I don't take the time to take care of these things, my creativity just isn't as joyful or fluid.

When I sat down earlier this year to begin the fundraising for *Boy Hero,* I gave myself a real honest pep talk. I was like, "Girl, if you don't learn to enjoy this part of the process real fast, what in heck are you even doing?" I knew I needed to find joy in the challenge, so I was going to have to make sure my personal cup was overflowing.

DESKTOP

I've said this for the longest time: sometimes I feel my brain is like a desktop, and its dashboard is something similar to the personality islands in the Pixar movie, *Inside Out.* On the bottom of my internal desktop is my "work brain". Each project gets its own folder that I can click on, and it keeps breaking down further from there.

This type of organization and maneuvering takes time to build. It took me years upon years of bumping into things and playing creative pinball to figure out where things belonged, what form goes where (and when), and what my specific order of operations should be.

These things take time both creatively and personally to develop, and usually they go hand-in-hand. Take your time to turn that computer off, but make sure to download so you can still collect new information. I cannot tell you how many times my mental desktop has frozen or been in overdrive.

A DAY OF NOTHING

Might I suggest to you a day of nothing? These are the most rewarding days. These are the days where your only job is to make no plans! I make myself have at least two of these a month where it's a complete blackout day; nothing written in my datebook, no one to meet, and no one that I have to take care of but myself. As you can see, I live my life nurturing and in service of others, so the days where I can keep that nurturing to myself is glorious. These days of nothing are so important in the grand scheme of things.

We want to be hungry to get back to work at the beginning of the week, or enjoy the process of a long day. Reward yourself with days of nothing. Making yourself do nothing is the most refreshing way to get yourself back to work the next day.

IT IS YOUR RESPONSIBILITY

At the end of the day, it becomes our responsibility to change our own lives if necessary. We've all been showered with different starting points based on family history, DNA, and social and economic upbringing. No matter what the chaos or the mess, there can be a way forward, and it comes back to taking action.

We should prioritize our mental health the way we might prioritize our projects, because let me tell you, we're all very much our own pieces of work, but we almost never do because we're always "too busy". I am a huge culprit of this. We get worried about finances and we're afraid to take an hour, or even a day off to help ourselves. I just want to encourage you that by putting mental health first, it really helps every other piece of the puzzle to fall into place.

I've wasted a lot of time in my past with a lot of worry and neurosis, and a lot of over thinking that would lead to a whole bunch of anxiety. We can help ourselves, become our own wells, and achieve inner peace. It's really cool that this can all come from an internal persistence, just the way that creating our own work can.

As we continue our journeys, I want to encourage you to allow this focus to remain at the top of your list. When the tragedies of life hit, the navigational practice of self-care and taking care of your mental health will be your life raft while you're under water. At some point, we will all crash and burn.

11

CRASH & BURN

Each of us have a period of extreme struggle in our lives. For many, that period has easily become 2020. A deadly pandemic reared its seething and ugly head, and at times it feels like it's had its way with all of us. This pandemic has left so many artists with a gaping hole and question mark of what's next.

For me, my "crash and burn" year was 2016. It was truly hell on earth. In the span of a month, I was dealt the worst hand imaginable. As you read previously, our amazing dad was taken from us way too soon after hearing five weeks prior that he had cancer. The great Ernie Adams passed away on August 20th, 2016.

If I think back, there were a few clues, but everyone always asked if there really weren't any major signs... No, not really, because my dad was a great actor. He never wanted to bother his family, or take extra days off of work to go to the doctor, even when he was hurting. I think the truth is that my dad was masking a lot of pain. On a day where his body couldn't help but give in, my Aunt Debbie called and told us he was laying on the floor in a lot of pain during a sitzprobe (a music rehearsal with the orchestra) of *Jesus Christ Superstar*. He was playing Pilot, a role deeply suited for him because of his stature, and permeating bass voice.

I remember that week he finally went to the doctor. The next few weeks were very murky, but for a short period of time, he was in and out of the hospital. Everything happened so quickly. Once we knew there was cancer in his body, there wasn't even enough time to set up a comfortable hospice for him at home, so he ended up back at the hospital.

It was horrible. The craziest thing is that because of a misreading of biopsies and a lack of understanding and communication, nobody ever realized how serious his condition actually was.

Our family had only *survived* cancer at this point. My resilient grandmother beat breast cancer twice before she passed from an infection, two years before my dad. Cancer is the worst, and it doesn't discriminate. It's a roulette game of DNA; the ball falling and landing in little pockets. There is no account taken if the person is good or not. Sometimes our heroes die, and they go out as loudly as they lived.

As if this weren't enough to navigate on its own, the world decided to give me another low blow in 2016. I was the lucky contestant who not only had won "the loss of my father" card, but I also received the double-whammy of what I still consider a major creative and business loss, as well.

I don't know how to write this other than to just... write it. It still baffles me that I allowed this to happen... but I *did* allow it, and I own that choice. Sometimes it's going to feel as though you've gotten yourself in too deep, and you just become paralyzed within a creative process. Forget the feeling of being drained, I mean, *paralyzed*.

You have read my words over the past few hours or days, and you have read over and over again me encouraging you to take your time within your creativity. So, I've got to say it again: you must *really* get to know people before you trust them with everything you have. Your stories and your personal experiences are included in this. I want to encourage you to use discernment. Well, my friends, when it came to my creative business as of 2016, I hadn't yet learned this gutting lesson. I shared my personal information and a very private idea to make a redemption story by turning some of the most challenging events from my childhood into a film. I made the decision to share this information with a person I'd known for only a few weeks.

We were working together at the time, and things were going smoothly. #BusinessBombersBeware in full effect. It was the whole "I'm learning how to produce movies" thing where, at the time, I knew I didn't know much about the medium, so I just took everything all in. I listened and worked, and while in the process of driving a truck full of equipment from Manhattan to Brooklyn to make my first union short film, I gave up way too much information, unprotected, way too fast.

The really sad part is that before I shared this information and idea I stated, "Now here's the deal, if I share this with you, you cannot take this and re-cast me with someone else. I'm telling this story to take my personal power back so I can play a version of myself in a more positive light."

After the words came out of me, I was promised with the immediate response, "Oh no, of course not. How would that even be possible? This movie could never happen without you."

So, I proceed to spill the beans. The idea was originally called *The Backlot*, and I'd already spoken about it with another writer/director who I'd previously lived with.

This person shared with me that they wanted to make their first feature film, and they also wanted to direct it. They were thinking, word for word, "Something gritty and dark, set in the south." Well, being the problem solver and creative I am, I got excited because I knew I had the answer to this person's wish. I had *my* story. And I decided to share it.

Just to be clear, this wasn't some creative idea I'd come up with, this was me sharing a personal story of something that happened to me in my childhood. I didn't journal, read a book, or have some life changing experience to inspire this idea. The sequence of events I told them had happened to me, and they happened to me as a *child*.

I am a survivor of sexual abuse. As a child, there was a teenage boy from my church family who did inappropriate things to me locked in a closet in rural Kentucky during a children's birthday party. Unfortunately, this teen also groomed and abused other young girls around my age within the church community, and at the end of the day, for numerous reasons, charges were not made in my own personal case.

It's important for me to state this in black and white, because with the production of the film that I inspired—through its release, premiere, and distribution—I never got that opportunity. That little girl was me, and she did more than survive. She moved to New York City alone, crossed off her childhood dream at 23, and then went on to create a massive opportunity to bring money back to the state of Kentucky to tell her redemption story. No one involved with the film really got the chance to know this back then, but you do, now.

I think what this person (who was hungry to make this film) did, was prey on and exploit my shame. When you're abused as a child, there's a certain shame you carry because you don't understand what happened to you, and because your own personal value was taken away on someone else's whim. You're left with that shame, because, "Who are you to draw attention to yourself by using your voice to say that what happened to you was wrong or inappropriate?"

These very things have been taken away from you because of the abuse, and it's uncomfortable to talk about. So, when you choose to make a film about it, if the correct environment isn't cultivated, the person who has already survived can easily be drawn back into that very same position.

I had finally used my voice. I shared this secret I'd been carrying for decades, and I wanted the film to be made, but I was told that as an actress I wasn't ready to carry a film of this nature. I was told by the person who was now directing the movie inspired by my life that I wasn't ready to play myself... and I believed it. We began with a few lessons, and I did everything requested of me because I always try to do things right. I've always been one to play by the rules. I was showing up to acting lessons with this director, growing, and not backing down. This was *my* redemption story, and I was going to tell it from a place of power.

Meanwhile, the packaging process had begun. I started rallying the troops in Louisville, cold calling everyone, sharing my story with speakerphones, and building out from the sides a team of allies to help make this dream come true. To me, it was worth it because my story was finally being shared.

I'd set up things pretty well for the film, and wasn't doing too bad for a green indie producer. I had attached some of my dearest friends to roles who had also come on to help me produce. I gathered people from my hometown, including the woman who'd sewn my prom dresses. She was the best local costume designer to help with wardrobe on set. We had gotten full support from the film commission (mainly because of my parents' previous relationships), and a bank account that was only in my name using my parent's home address so that we could begin our production in Kentucky. Now this is very important to note: the assets, legal pieces, and responsibility of the LLC were in my name, but by this time I had, by choice and in complete ignorance, signed over full creative control to the director. Yep. That happened. I did that. Originally, there were four producers on this film, but just like my lead role, in a little over a year's time, both of those people had been removed from the film.

Once again, because I was still learning, I was told this kind of thing happens all the time, and the most important thing for me was to see the film get made. This whole process simply wasn't jiving with my soul—they were burning bridges left and right just to see a piece of art get made. Now, with the trauma I had previously experienced in my personal life on the subject, I absolutely wanted the film to be made at this point, so I went with the flow. It was draining. But now I gladly took up space in the table reads and pitch materials as a "supporting female character with a heart of gold" in the film. My 'safety' role, which I had now moved into by 'choice'.

The production literally continued to go south. Every step forward began to feel increasingly uncomfortable, like I wasn't in the right place, even though this creative process was born from me. Things were not matching up. People that I'd brought into our film family were being taken advantage of, and I wasn't having any piece of it. I knew I'd gotten in way too deep, and that I was slowly becoming paralyzed. My creativity or opinion, at this point, was null and void. Forget any basic human respect that should have been given for sharing my story; that wasn't even on the radar. How do you remove yourself from something that is *yours?* Something that is *your* story, but that's started to morph into something that no longer feels like home? You just... do. It's never too late to turn around, no matter how deep you may have gone in that direction, and no matter the cost of what you might be giving up in the process.

It was excruciating. It took me months of reflection before I was ready to say I could no longer condone or take legal responsibility for this property. My bottom line had been reached. This experience, a year-and-a-half in, did not fall under any part of me, my values, my practices, or my ways of doing business, so I made the really challenging decision to let this other energy completely take over the project. They now had full reign in telling my story. I signed a lifetime rights agreement to give that away. There was shame because this had now become a part of my story. I was learning the painful lesson that no project is worth your peace of mind, or your integrity. Nothing is worth selling your integrity. Your dreams and your time will come.

So, I now had to begin to negotiate and fight to keep any credit. In the film inspired by my life, I had to fight for a co-producer credit, and a title at the beginning of the film. My lawyer at the time on another project asked me if I wanted him to step in and shut it down, but as a survivor, I'd already done the hardest part: I had bravely shared my story. I wanted to allow the production to continue, and I didn't want the actors to be affected, or be made to feel uncomfortable at all. To this day, these folks don't know that I was originally supposed to have been on screen opposite them, or the woman who made this opportunity happen for them. Zero clue. I chose to go with grace to create a professional work environment for all.

In the end, I didn't even get to be in the movie inspired by my life story. I was replaced in my secondary 'safety' role the day after I transferred ownership. The craziest thing is that I saw the director that afternoon by chance in midtown, on their way to meet a mutual friend who was going to personally introduce them to the woman who was going to replace me in the role. The universe allowed me to see these things with my own eyes because it knew I was going to have a lot to swallow, and have to let go.

I flew out to the premiere in LA even though I knew I wasn't going to be acknowledged in the press line. I was emotionally prepared for this. At the event, one of our executive producers grabbed me and pushed me towards the step and repeat. He stated so proudly, "This is *your* movie," as the press flashed their cameras. "This is the woman the movie was based on!" I was grateful for the acknowledgement.

At the premiere's Q&A, I watched as each member of the cast and crew were called down to the front. There were about 30 people. I wasn't even mentioned. And when it was asked how this powerful film idea came about, he said, "It was born at a Christmas party." That's totally how it happened, right?

I had flown to Los Angeles alone because I had just recently lost my father. My family wasn't in the place to travel and come out to support me on this extremely hard night, so I sat there alone, feeling like I was having an out of body experience. But my father's spirit was with me. I will never forget that feeling. I will never forget watching the film inspired by my own life, not having been given any acknowledgement for opening up my soul. In that moment, I had learned exactly what type of creative I didn't want to become, no matter what the cost. While the film was in my hometown shooting at the locations I had secured, my father was dying in the hospital.

I don't know if this story could have gotten any worse. It is what it is. It's in the hand that I was dealt so that I can be here now, wiser, more aware, and more grounded and connected with you. I am proud that both this film and story were shared before—and helped lead up to—the #MeToo movement.

The good people sniffed me out and asked where I'd gone. There were a few who realized that I'd been so present in the beginning, but had slowly disappeared by the end. The right people always notice these things and always ask questions, regardless of you keeping your mouth shut. Truth always finds its way out. I appreciate the people who took the time to put the pieces together and come to me. As I said to the person whose journey it became, I will always be proud of the finished film, but I will never be proud of its process.

Sometimes life kicks us down. Sometimes everything we have is taken away from us and burned, all at the same time. And why? I do believe this happens to some of us who are supposed to get kicked down, who are supposed to experience grief, death, sadness, pain, and longing, so that we may come back and prevail. So that we can come back, grow into clearer storytellers, and share our stories to help heal and encourage others.

It's only after these harrowing experiences that we learn how strong we truly are, how brave we are, and what we're actually capable of. These are the losses of life that mold our every breath, hope, and dream. We have been to hell and back with these pains, and many times have seen the devils face in others' actions and choices, or have lived within our greatest nightmares.

To all who are holding this book: that horrible thing that has happened to you, or that was taken away from you right under your nose... do not let it discourage you. Do not allow it to stop you. I promise you that your time will come. I promise that you will be seen for everything you have ever given. I promise you people will hear your story and know it's yours. And who knows, maybe it will be told in a different medium like this story has been shared with you here today.

Even when we unknowingly crash and burn, we must get back up. We must prevail. We must breathe again. We must find the courage to stand back up and to continue creating. And this time, we will heal, and we will fly higher than ever before.

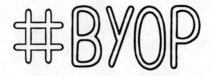

CHALLENGES FOR PART THREE: ACTION

#BYOP CHALLENGE 11:
WORK BEGETS WORK

1. Make a list of action steps, big and small, for your new creative idea or small business.
2. Label the smaller goals 'immediate' and the larger ones "big picture".
3. Give yourself some deadlines for both! (I usually have a to-do list for the week and then one for each season or quarter)
4. Begin attacking your immediate goals today, and create a schedule for the big picture goals. Spend at least a work day a week focused on those bigger picture goals while knocking off the smaller goals for some instant gratification and speedy progress.
5. Get creative to intersect the immediate and big picture goals. Your time can serve both at the same time!
6. Schedule, reset and repeat! This work will create energy, and work only begets more work!

#BYOP CHALLENGE 12:
REVISITING & REVAMPING OLDER IDEAS

1. Now that you have a better understanding of how your current idea might be structured or explored, let's take a look back on some of your older ideas that you wrote down and might have really connected with in the past.

2. Do any of these older ideas serve as inspiration to you now? Do they maybe have content that you can pull from to solve a current problem? If so, give yourself a pat on the back!

3. Now that you have a better infrastructure, are there any older ideas or inspirations that you might want to add to your bigger picture list? Try not to sleep on those original instinct ideas!

4. Like anything, give yourself time to reflect on bringing this older idea to the forefront, and make sure you have the current capacity to bring it into the mix.

#BYOP CHALLENGE 13:
CLARIFY CREDIT

1. If collaboration is a part of your current artistic venture, make a Google or Word Doc that explains each member of your creative team, their titles and duties, expectations, and payment with deadlines.

2. Make sure there is documentation and agreements that reflect these choices. (An email or simple deal memo is fine if you don't have access to a lawyer. There just has to be something to protect yourself from business bombers before you get in too deep!)

3. If you aren't ready to jump into creative business with someone, take the time on the front end to get everything in

order before you share all of your content or ideas with the people you're planning to collaborate with.

4. If you need to share information or content with someone to see how they might fit into the puzzle, you can always provide them with an NDA (non-disclosure agreement) before you have that initial conversation.

5. Make sure your content is registered or copyrighted if applicable.

6. Discuss as much as you can up front so it saves you from really uncomfortable conversations later. This might include (but not limited to) the possibility of future expansion, brand extensions, and adding additional team members. These can all be a part of that initial brainstorm conversation.

#BYOP CHALLENGE 14:
TAKE CONSISTENT INVENTORY

1. Now that you've gotten further into the process of expanding your creative business, are there any red flags that stand out to you?

2. Take time to write down those flags and discuss strategy with your team (or your favorite imposter busters) as to how you can get things in line together. You can solve multiple problems, but you have to give yourself the time to assert them. Face it all ASAP!

3. Are there any people who you're currently collaborating with that aren't exactly matching up with your values or the way you do business? If so, what about these transactions are making you feel uncomfortable?

4. Have that challenging conversation. Rip off the Band-Aid and see if some fusing or healing can happen between you and that party.

5. Is there anyone in your path that still isn't fitting after a period of trying to fix it from all sides? Do you feel that reconciliation might not be possible? Is this working relationship still serving both parties, or do you both feel held back? If so, it might be time to go with grace.

#BYOP CHALLENGE 15:
TAKE CARE OF #1

1. What are the things you know you need in order to fill up your cup both mentally and emotionally?

2. How are you currently asserting your self-care right now?

3. What do you feel might be missing?

4. Do you feel it might help you to have professional support? If so, high five! Welcome to the club. Seeking professional help is the best decision I've ever made for myself, and my sanity and creativity.

5. If you know you're feeling overwhelmed, revisit #BYOP Challenge #9!

6. Give yourself a BREAK!

#BYOP CHALLENGE 16:
HEALING WITH THE HOPE OF THE PHOENIX:

1. If you found this challenge while going through a personal or business crisis, I am so deeply sorry. It sucks. There is no graceful way to state it, and for that, I'm sorry. Just trust me in knowing that over time, and with the help of your

personal and creative support system, this will get better. Or at least easier to swallow.

2. Take time to sign off. Delegate or communicate your need for space, reflection, or time. Get it out of the way so you can focus on what is most important right now, which is your healing and reflection.

3. Sit in it. This is the worst part, but it's also the most necessary for proper healing. Take time for reflection and inventory. This process will help you heal the most. Up your doses of self-care during this extremely uncomfortable time.

4. Was this situation preventable? If so, what could you have done different so that when presented with this situation again, there might be a better result? Remember those things because there will be a next time.

5. Allow yourself to get angry. When digesting hard moments or news, I struggle with this the most because I try to only be productive, and for me, anger never feels like a 'productive' emotion. But I try to remind myself that it can be. You *will* do better next time.

6. Try to forgive yourself. This one might take a lot of time. Remember, you're learning and building towards a brighter future.

7. Take your time when getting back up. Allow yourself some grace.

8. When the time is right, you'll know it in your soul, and you will rise back up wiser and braver than before. You can do this! Look back at how far you've come. You have survived everything up until this point, and you will fly once again! I believe in you!

#BYOP

PART FOUR

BE YOUR OWN PRODUCER

12

HEAL & CARRY ON

When we have fallen into the lowest of lows and lost everything, how do we heal? How do we actually stand back
up? How do we get up off of the ground and attempt to
continue again? Where do we even find the desire to continue
again? In life, there are so many pressures. Life can be so loud,
and can move at such a rapid pace. And when you experience
a loss (personally or in your career), you are truly standing still
within the circus of monkeys. We have to value ourselves and our
journeys enough to take the time we need. That's the number one
thing people will say to you after the loss of an immediate family
member—take all of the time that you need—and I am here to tell
you that you must take it.

Grief is otherworldly. Of all the experiences my body and soul have been through, grief is by far the craziest. It completely takes over—all the while your entire being has no other choice but to go along for the ride. You, humble human, can't control what comes next in your process. A few years ago, I wrote a poem that I shared on the first anniversary of my father's passing about feeling like I was a boat, locked into a dock at sea, and that I had no choice but to remain attached to this dock and ride out the storm, praying for the calm, sunny days to come.

The process of digesting and dissecting your pain, loss, or curveball can become extremely tedious. I've tried to get comfortable in my losses. I will never be comfortable *experiencing* the feelings that come with that loss, but I'm more aware now, and therefore more comfortable receiving it.

There are so many lessons to receive in grief. The pain that we feel in a loss will be the reflection of the love that was there within that relationship. Who was that person to you? Your grief will be as loud as your loss. When I lost my father, I knew it was going to take me out for a while. And it did. It was crucial that I took my time. My dad was worthy of that time, and so was I.

The timing of my two simultaneous losses were almost comedic in their heaviness. I couldn't believe that I had to be kicked while I was down. But it was my story, so I had to face it. Sitting in it is truly the only way out and through.

SIT IN IT

When we're experiencing the lowest points of our life, we must try to do so with our eyes open. I don't know how we have the magical power to overcome, but every one of us does possess these skills, no matter how hard the circumstances are to get back up. But that rise up doesn't happen overnight. We have to sit in our grief. We have to sit in, and acknowledge our personal or creative loss. We have to feel it all.

While I was battling through this, I reached out to things that healed me. For me, time alone became necessary. I would say before my father passed that I considered myself 90% an extrovert. I hardly ever gave myself time to be alone and recharge, but since then, I have become much more of an introvert. As I said to my friend the other day, I feel that I'm a good 60/40 now. I need time to digest things now, and this is a good thing! For a person who didn't always use discernment when making exciting or spontaneous decisions, this was a gift and a lesson found within my grief. I also did a lot of yoga to help my body feel better. I leaned into Vinyasa during the week, and on the weekends, I would allow myself to recharge with restorative yoga. I needed that comfort, and because of it, yoga has become a part of my consistent physical and spiritual routine.

I want to also encourage you to find the comfort of your friends. For my friend group, the passing of my dad was uncharted territory. I was the first to "join the club", as I've heard other young people refer to the loss of a parent. None of us knew what we were doing, or how to be. I was challenged to really articulate my needs for the first time in my life, and we all attempted to face it as a group. I have the best girlfriends in the world. They helped to lift me up to the light and to ease the pain when the only way through was sitting in it.

Remember when we were talking about the things you needed to take note of that help you to fill up your cup? In these most challenging moments of life is where those things become so important. We need to know what makes our bodies and souls feel better.

Though I hope that you reach for healthy things that can positively create new life within you during your time of need. Even in our healing, the creation of life's personal journey never stops.

GRIEF AND PRODUCTIVITY

Since my father's passing, I have learned to become friends with my grief. If I can tell you a secret, about three years ago I had the desire to write a book about grief for younger people. I noticed one didn't really exist, and I wanted to aid people in having this very specific conversation if they were in need of it. When you're navigating that type of engulfing grief, your entire being is swallowed by it for years and years. And for me, the vortex of grief still consistently opens up on major anniversary dates related to my father's passing.

When grieving a massive loss, you become a new person. Every single belief system or idea of life is challenged, and you spend the amount of energy that you've experienced loving another human, now grieving their sudden disappearance. That's literally what it feels like; they're there one day, and they aren't the next. Our bodies, hearts, and spirits have to navigate this cruel magic trick of mortality, and watch how it begins to inform every movement, choice, and breath. *Everything* hurts when you are grieving.

Before my father passed, I *thought* I'd grieved before, but like my first panic attack, I didn't know what it was called. I'm almost certain I grieved the sudden closing of my Broadway show, which I shared with you in the foreword. It wasn't one-tenth as impactful as the loss of my father, but it absolutely was a response of grief, as it affected my ideals, mood, and behavior. It's interesting though, my grief has always been paired with a type of shock attached to it. Everything (and everyone) I have ever lost has been extremely sudden and unexpected. And that adds a double layer of trauma to the grief, because you've got to learn to navigate it before you can even step into the main event. It's truly wacky, y'all. Truly.

While it wasn't my calling to write an entire book on grief at the moment, through my struggles I learned that it was a part of my calling to speak on grief and how it can inform our creativity. When the pandemic hit, this need came in full swing.

As #BYOP began to expand, I did a series on grief and productivity. It's okay if when you're grieving you don't feel like creating. Your grief is having the most authentic creative experience inside you, and I promise that's enough. It's permeating every fiber of your being, and you never know exactly where it will go. Like your creativity, it's completely unpredictable and original to you and your experiences. The range of emotion is shocking, terrifying, and more informative than any prestigious drama program in the country. Like birth, death (and grief) is the other pinnacle of life, and it'll have its way with you no matter what your wishes are.

We simply have to ride it out and let the waves of grief wash over us. We also must give ourselves the days, months, or even years to allow this process to take place. Let sadness, loss, and grief take center stage, or it'll always be slowly creeping back in, trying to yank you off your own center stage with a cane.

THE LESSONS OF LOSS

When we grieve, we lose our facilities and aren't as clear headed or sharp, so the adaptive energy just drips out of our soul and body, leaving us empty almost every single day. Just yesterday, I barreled through an anniversary date of my father's passing, and once again it was extremely loud. But in some ways this pain can become a gift. I've heard that blessings can be found in grief. To me, the blessings I found were the lessons I learned.

For the first time in my life I was forced to do additional inventory. Thank God I had an active therapist, and that the inventory process had already begun years before; this was like phase two on overdrive. It all began again. I had to learn how to live again. At times it felt like I had to learn how to walk again, or to take a deep breath again. I would think, pray, meditate, and write down my pain on this. What did I need? What was I hearing? What were the lessons?

My lesson became loud and clear. I needed to truly value myself. And this lesson, although it's one of the first things I worked on with my therapist years prior, became the key to the next steps of my future, in every single lane of my life. I was truly ready to live in this lesson. I had taken plenty of baby steps towards living in this lesson, but now was the time to allow it to repaint my black and white world. I got to step back into technicolor with Dorothy, and this time it was going to be a true party.

Holding onto my larger lesson and asserting it was one of the things that began to inform my fire of getting back up. I had work to do. I had boundaries to set, dead weight I needed to drop, and I had an entire life that I needed to take inventory of. The fire slowly started to burn again and I began to start anew.

BUSINESS BETRAYALS AND TAKING SPACE

In addition to loss, I had to process a betrayal of my business with others. Because I wasn't taking my time in the development phases of projects to understand the heart and intention of others, I was forced to process the aftermath. I'd been left with such an incomplete closure of something that had once meant so much to me, and it made me learn to let go of something that felt so personal. I also had to take a break from collaboration for a bit to protect my he(art).

If you feel like you want to take space in order to reassert where you're going in the next step of your creative career, I want to encourage you to take it. Like with a personal loss, there is an idea of life, an idea of development, or an idea of working relationship that you might have to grieve before you feel you're ready to open yourself back up to others in collaboration again.

I took my time. I developed my next projects quietly and privately, and then began asking all of the red flag questions I'd gathered from my first years of work. These challenges and painful mistakes informed who I wanted to collaborate with during this next season. I went almost completely in the opposite direction by using my discernment. For my screenplay, I've only shared it with private creative personal contacts, or a handful of people who were highly recommended from sources I am actively working with today. (That would be you, Mr. Zach Spicer of Pigasus Pictures, and you, Miss Alli Ryan of AR Productions). It's been a great strategy, and has allowed me to heal completely and step back in so I can help lead fearlessly once again. No matter how strong we are, the healing process takes time. You are worthy of taking this time to understand where you have come from to then assert where you're going.

PRIORITIZE THE PRESSURES

When I am overwhelmed, I prioritize the pressures. Whenever I feel like I'm about to crawl out of my skin with responsibilities, I remember to take a deep breath. We spoke earlier in the book about the idea of rational vs. irrational challenges, and how sometimes our inner dramatics or life experience can inform irrational thoughts or feelings within ourselves. This is when that weight seems too heavy. When you're healing, you just have to center yourself with what actually needs to get done, and then attempt to delegate or give yourself permission from the rest.

When I needed space to heal both personally and in my creative business, I cut out all of the extraneous things. You only have the capacity for the bare essentials because all of your adaptive energy is gone from dealing with life.

During this process of rebuilding, I want to encourage you to prioritize what actually must be done like paying your bills, making sure you're showing up to work, keeping connected with your loved ones and helpers, and doing simple tasks at home like laundry and taking out the garbage. We have to be able to do those things before we add the additional pressures of being the revolutionary and ground breaking creative that we are. Know what I mean?

PRESSING PAUSE ON YOUR PROJECT

Throughout this book, we've been focusing on cultivating an idea, project, or story that we know we need to tell. But sometimes, because of larger than life circumstances, we have to press pause on our projects no matter where they might be.

Your project will let you know what you need to do with it for the time being. Sometimes you're in the middle of a process and your body will literally carry you to the next goal post of the project, finding the best place to stop and rest for the moment. Sometimes you might have to ask someone else to carry the torch for you for a while. I have had to do both.

Your current state will inform how you need to take action briefly so you can then press pause. I always want to encourage you to communicate the need to take time and space. People will understand, but you have to let them know so they can do what they need to do to help you organize and keep this project afloat.

THE PHOENIX

Listen to me, my creative friend: you will rise again. There is no obstacle that's too big to overcome and heal from that you cannot face head on. You know this by now: sometimes life flat out sucks. This has become a given for many of us, but I promise that everything we've lost or have had taken away from us, can—and will—inform our future. You hold the power, even when you have lost it. We become like a phoenix, rising out of the ashes, and we will soar again.

You know that authenticity you've been searching for? That massive piece within your identity? This is the crux that informs the entirety of you and your creativity. Your new normal. It's going to inform your work, your projects and content, and your working relationships and how you relate to others. It'll inform this fiery, unstoppable, clear headed and focused phoenix that you have become.

A few of my best friends brought up the idea of a phoenix to me when I told them I was going to dive into writing this book. My therapist even mentioned it to me yesterday when I told her I was close to finishing the first draft! As you've read, this book is the culmination and companion to all of the most joyful and painful lessons throughout my creative journey thus far, to hopefully encourage more ease in your own. I hope you have taken my tips and tricks, and scooped up your own red flags along the way. If you take anything from these pages, I want you to know that you can, and will prevail amongst all odds. If I can do it blindly, you too can be your own producer. So, are you ready to take the biggest #BYOP Challenge of your life?

13

#BYOP

Being your own producer is acknowledging and embracing your own personal resilience. Using all of your gifts, life experiences, joys, and tragedies, and using that to push you up the mountains of your wildest dreams. It's the process of getting back up, the awareness and ability to acknowledge that you *can* start over again and again, and the awareness to know where you've been along your journey. You've done your homework enough to move your own pendulum and know where you're going because you get to choose your next destination. You don't wait around for anyone to tell you what's next because you begin to move first. You have *everything* inside of you! You have always had these abilities! With this book—plus your natural gifts, stories, calling, and workflow—you now have the main ingredients in creating your own glorious journey.

It all comes back to you, your hopes and dreams, and what burns inside you that you *must* share with this world. The world needs your perspective, it needs your expression, and it needs your stories. You've already proven to yourself that you have everything you need to be your own producer.

I celebrate your resilience. I celebrate your deeper desire to connect and take your space. I celebrate your acute awareness, and the moments when you choose to take a step back and to listen. Today we celebrate YOU! We celebrate your creativity, and your own personal creative process!

THE PREMIERE

If you have made it this far to see your project fully shift from idea to completion, you have truly witnessed a miracle! Look at how many twists, turns, and emotions you've navigated while remaining steady. Look at what you committed to through all of the unknown. Finally, look at what you've built.

If you have the privilege of sharing your complete (or complete enough) work with others on a big screen, in a transaction on Etsy, or in a reading or onstage, *rejoice* in this moment. No process or project will ever be the same again. Rejoice in working with your group of chosen humans, all banning together to pull off something truly rare and astonishing.

Thank your team and celebrate them in your gratitude. Use your words. Explain to people what you couldn't have done without them. You experienced their grace, their assistance, and their help, so be sure to tell them that and to acknowledge them. I promise that gratitude will go the longest way and holds the ability to create "forever teams".

Have fun. Try to take the moment in. Attempt to be fully present throughout all of the jitters. Try to remember the look on people's faces and the hugs. Take as many pictures as you can get. Try to remember these things for when you need it as encouragement to get you through your next process or project.

The best thing is, if we've completed a process once, we know it can (and will) happen again if we put our heart and mind to it. If we have overcome once before, we know we can do it again, and again, and again. Your proof is right there in front of you.

IT ONLY STOPS IF YOU DO

Our creativity, work, and our careers will only stop if we do. We now know our preferred way to create. Our favorite way to make money may at times might be unexpectedly taken away from us, but that doesn't mean our creativity is dead. We are still living. We can push ourselves to explore other lanes, and there we might even find additional gifts that can pair with the others to create a longevity in the arts! We have now realized how inventive we truly are. I promise that inside of you there are multiple untapped ideas or inklings that have the ability to create more stability than any booking or contract could ever give you- more than you ever realized. You will continue to live and create; there is only more where that came from.

If you continue to show up for yourself and others consistently, that work is going to *flow!* There is no other option! The projects you've cultivated and made with your most honest energy and purpose will only stop if you do.

CELEBRATE BEING SELF-SUFFICIENT

When we take on #BYOP clients, the goal is to share tools, methods, and lessons for them to become self-sufficient. I really want you to have the ability to become your very own producer! Maybe I am the worst consultant and producer in the world. I'm never going to pretend like I hold all the answers. All I can do is to encourage you to uncover your own answers through a process that works best for you, and cheer you on from the sidelines. When we produce our own work, we have to become our own problem solvers. The more often we can efficiently make challenging decisions on our own, the more fluid our production or creative process becomes.

One of my favorite self-sufficient problem solvers is OG #BYOP client, Emm O' Connor. She has literally become her own producer since working together! She and her creative/business partner, Jim Mauro have just celebrated three years as Viridian Coast Studios, LLC. After the success of *Capital Advice,* they continued their collaboration while working for major network shows like *The Chew,* and *Full Frontal with Samantha Bee.* They developed and shot another original concept and script by Emm, called *Brewtown,* and developed and shot a series called *Under the Influence,* created by Tara Llewellyn. They are incredible and resilient human beings who I'm proud to call colleagues and friends.

I AM SO PROUD OF YOU

To our #BYOP clients and readers: look at this journey you've allowed yourself to take! Look at some of the things you uncovered and what you're starting to take space from. Look at the glaring red flags that you're finally ready to let go of and drop the dead weight. Look at your authentic creativity and the projects that will come of it. I am truly *so* proud of you.

Take pride in pushing yourself to know *you* better and how you work. These are the processes that add to your internal value and allow your personal character to shine through in your art and creativity. Unleash your true calling and revamp the things that may have previously felt disconnected. Let them have it! Let the world see your most honest and reflective expressions! Unleash your truth!

FLUID CREATIVITY

The doors have finally been removed and you now have permission to freely roam throughout the entire house of your creative energy—guided by your impulses, truth, and reflection. You get to experience riding the wave of your now fluid creativity.

Acknowledge as you leave these pages how your creativity continues to move. Continue to take inventory of what motivates you, what inspires you, and what pulls out your curiosity and passions. Those are your answers. Enjoy painting with more joy, singing with intention, and building with grace. Enjoy the dance of your authentic creativity. Enjoy doing it all, and watch how it nurtures both you and others. I can't wait to see what you've made.

STAY CONNECTED

Please be sure to share your journeys and triumphs with us. We want to celebrate you and share your creative work and expressions since you're now a part of our creative tribe! See how that works? We're always working on ways to stay connected both in person and virtually, and we'll always be sure to inform you of those future opportunities.

You can share your work with us on Instagram by tagging @byop_nyc or @ashleykateadams, and we WILL share it and support you. Our team is also available to work with you one-on-one through your own creative process, project, or even through the conversation of processing this book! www.ashleykateadams.com will always be the home for this information, no matter how much my personal creativity might shift or change. We will always have your back, and our team will always cheer you on!

THE #BYOP CHALLENGE

The biggest #BYOP challenge is here. It's finally that time for me to encourage you from afar as you continue thriving, growing, and building. You've done the hardest part by taking inventory and being brutally honest with yourself and others about your creativity. You have taken your time. You have not left any rock unturned, and you are prepared.

And now...drumroll please! Your official #BYOP Challenge of the book is to remain open to doing this process again, and again, and again. That will be the biggest #BYOP Challenge of all. Always do this type of work regardless of your success or failures, and I promise with time it will become routine within your life. We never outgrow our present identity, ideas, inspirations, and actions. You and your creativity are boundless because you *are* your creativity. You have the ability to be your own producer again, and again. You hold the courage to translate any season of life onto the page or screen. You hold the power to answer many of your own questions and respond to your greatest worries and fears. You have the power to ask for guidance when it's all too much. You are your own generator of purpose and possibility.

So, go on now! Be your own producer. Be your own producer of content, of creativity, of happiness, and OF YOUR FUTURE. I cannot wait to see what you create, express, and share, and how you help to elevate and inspire others in our world.

IN DEEPEST GRATITUDE

I am so happy to have the opportunity to thank the following people in print who may or may not have been mentioned yet in this book. I am thankful to each and every single one of you, and deeply grateful for the love and energy you have shared with me throughout my life. Without you, this leap would not have been possible.

Thank you to my direct team for this book. Thank you to my dear friend and AKA Studio Productions teammate, **Kristen Seavey**, for taking the time to edit these words to where it allowed my soul to shine through all of my bumps and bruises. You have the most generous heart and abilities, and I could not have imagined these words in the care of anyone but you. Thank you. Thank you to my little queen, **Lauren Lebowitz**, who vibes with the light of #BYOP unlike anyone else. Thank you for believing in the big picture and showing it to me literally on paper. I wake up every day excited that you share the same love for this project as I do. I am grateful that you are a big piece of my team. **Kate Anderson-Song**, thank you for your consistency and gentleness that always gives me courage. As we have grown over the past few years, I wouldn't have been able to complete all of my passions at once without your understanding, and fellow creative fluidity and support. Thank you for your kindness, and thank you for your belief in where we are going. To my creative brother **Patryk Larney**: my friend, you are always my translator. Thank you for cheering me on and collaborating with me through my career, this book, and for making it look amazing. If it was not for you introducing me to the brilliant **Jeff Hammer**, this book would not be real. Thank you both for believing in my bigger dreams and potential. **Ailsa Hoke**, I have known you the longest of my teammates and our deepest selves connect us, our upbringing, and our greatest losses. I am honored to have your light and expertise encouraging the way of this book. Laura and Ernie are deeply proud of what we have become. To **David Hancock** and my team at **Morgan James Publishing**, thank you for publishing my first book and for sharing similar interests and values with me. Thank you for giving me a platform to use my voice and share my heart.

To my literary agent, **Amy Wagner** of A3 Artists Agency, thank you for seeing me for all of my creativity and helping me find a true home for it. Thank you for helping me to organize my full value, and for encouraging me to write and produce new works. Thank you for being the first person to tell me I must write this book. To my theatrical team at A3 (**Richard Fisher, Robert Atterman, Samantha Stoller, Danielle DeLawder, Robyn Rosen, Paul Reisman**), and to my previous managers (**Chase**

Jennings, Stevie Smith, Edie Robb), thank you for helping me to open the first doors in my acting career that have brought me to this place. Your belief in me helped me to create my foundation and home in New York City. Thank you for cheering me on even in every corner of my creativity. I am so excited to see how all of these lanes continue to merge!

To my current teammates and the OG's of AKA Studio Productions: thank you so much for believing in the possibilities as our interests and creativity started to shift and take shape a decade ago. **Ari Wilford**, thank you for starting this journey with me in 2011 and helping me to take hold of my disbelief and to turn it into productive energy. Thank you for being one of my very best friends and confidants. I love you deeply my friend. **Emily Ryan**, I am thankful for you being my original support through the forward motion years of AKA. You are one of my dearest friends and I am so happy we still are collaborating today within our latest experiences. I also must give a big thank you to **Janine Lee Papio**. Without your deep belief in me I would not have arrived so presently here today. Thank you for helping me push AKA to the next level through our original cornerstone projects, and helping me to build the foundation as to where the company would be heading next. Remember our other original consulting project? My how we have grown gracefully into our dreams. And to my go-to imposter buster, dear friend, and fellow producer, **Mitchell Walker**, we have gone "John and Tonya" style together for the past 15 years. I hope you are LIVING DREAMS because we are stuck together baby! I love you dearly, and I am so grateful we get to share so much.

Thank you again to my family. My how great of an honor it is to be an Adams. To my mom **(Dana "Hoe" Jo Adams)** and departed daddy-o **(Ernie Adams)**, this book has been for you. All

I have ever wanted to do was make you proud. It was the greatest gift to be born of your love and creativity. I hope sharing my stories and experiences have brought you even more pride. Thank you, Mom, for being the best mom. Thank you for being the best example that a woman can help lead in and outside of the home. Your strength and grace are unparalleled. I am so happy to be so close to you in this season of my life. To my little brother, **Wesley Chace Adams**, thank you for being my OG best friend, my brother bear, and for demonstrating a love of learning and books to me. Growing up you were the reader in the family and the one who could finish any storyline whether it be written or within a video game at lightning speed because of your sheer brilliance. Thank you for always being proud of me. I am excited to see where your knowledge continues to take you. To my little sister, **Audrey Belle Adams**, one of my greatest inspirations and deepest confidants, thank you for your unwavering belief and support in me. Loving you so deeply and my pride in you has better taught me how to take pride in myself. You give me courage. I am in awe of your gifts, talents, and your strength. Thank you for your unwavering belief in my creative explorations. I love you and I am so proud of your current accomplishments. I am SO excited for your future. To my **Aunt Debbie Hutchison**, everyone's favorite "Aunt Debbie", thank you for always nurturing mindfulness in my life and development before it was culturally a thing. Your gentleness and awareness helped to guide me as I grew up and to help me find strength in my transparency, emotions and sensitivities. Without your love, I would not be the woman I am today and I guarantee I would not have expanded into all of my lines of nurturing work. I love you. To **"Morgie" Hutchison**, thank you for always cheering me on. I think you were the closest person to me who I got to try out my pep talks with. I am so proud of your resilience and the ways that you love. Thank you for always cheering me on and for ALWAYS understanding what I am trying to do or say. I am so excited to continue to collaborate with you on projects and your wedding. To my **Grandpa Adams**, the best reader and the greatest guy we all know, thank you for leading our family so steadfastly with so much grace. You have lived an extraordinary life of 91 years! You have taught us all how to love deeply and have shown me the fun in fixing and building things from an early age. I really hope you have gotten a kick out of reading your first grandchild's published book. To my aunts and uncles (**Randy and Judy, Gary and Paul, Leon and Lisa, Wayne and Paula, Robbie and Kim**), thank you for always loving and supporting me and my dreams! I am thankful for my loving family. To my grandma, **Edith Swinford**, who has passed, thank you for helping to raise me and show me how to be a strong working woman and to love music. I feel the way I move through life has so much of you in it. To my sweet and nurturing grandma, **Joan Adams**, I try to always exude the gentleness of you. Thank you for sharing your nurturing spirit with me so I can love on others. To **Jim Swinford**, my "Pop Pop", thank you for demonstrating joy and laughter to my upbringing. I would always be the most excited to see you and to spend time with you growing up. I also learned resilience and humility from you. I am very proud to be your granddaughter.

To my very best friends who are also my family, I could not do life without each and every single one of you. I am so thankful for your consistency, love and support in my life. To my OG besties from my adolescence: **Misty Davis, Patrick Martin,** and **Paige Quiggins**. Boy how lucky are we to still be sharing life since high school ended? I love you all and thank you for being my first unwavering chosen family members. To **"Benny Boo" Ochsner**, thank you for being my personal Imposter Buster and best friend. I am so thankful we have gotten to grow up together as a team. I am always so proud of you and your creativity. I love you. To my college besties **Kristin Moore, James Lee Glatz** and **Alessa Neeck**, I am so thankful that my deepest friendships and support from some of the most disciplined years of our lives translated into lifelong friendships. I love each of you deeply and take deep pride in each of you. Thank you for always helping me to keep my head above water. To my best friends that I have made in New York City, I don't know what I would do without you. **Remy Zaken, Kate Loprest, Caitlin Cooke, Courtney Leigh Halford, Lauren "LOLO" Pritchard** and **Alli Ryan Motley**, you are my soul sisters. We have all shared so much together and I am grateful that I get to share the corners of my life with you. Thank you all for being my unwavering family, stooo-ning cheerleaders and for celebrating life's most exciting moments and expansions with me and standing firmly beside me in the loss of my father. Thank you for helping me shine every day.

To my therapist, **Dr. T**, thank you for showing me the best commitment I could ever make is to myself. Thank you for seven years of reflection and for challenging me lovingly and for celebrating the steps I have taken. Thank you for being my greatest confidant and cheerleader. The generosity of your spirit is unparalleled.

And speaking of generous spirits, this brings me to my final thank you that I have for now, my love and my future, **Joe Cosmo Cogen**. There are no words to truly describe my gratitude for you. Thank you for re-entering my life—it was most certainly ordained by the cosmos. I have never felt support and unconditional love from anyone the way I have found this match in you. Every day gets to be a celebration of love, creativity, family and dreams with you. You are the dreamiest of all of the dreamboats, and I thank you for loving me and being my partner. Who would have ever known life inside a pandemic could be so joyful and safe? Thank you for giving me space to write this book while sheltering in place with me. Thank you for making sure I have eaten my lunch, and for making more than half of them as I'm down the rabbit hole. Thank you for creating a loving home with me, and for taking as much pride and joy in our dinner time as I do. Thank you for being my safe place. I love you, and I thank you for loving me. I can't wait to share the rest of my life with you.

I thank you all. Now let's CELEBRATE!

ABOUT THE AUTHOR

Ashley Kate Adams was born and raised in Louisville, Kentucky, and is now a New York City based award-winning actress and producer who made her Broadway debut at the age of 23 in the Tony Award winning revival of *La Cage Aux Folles*. She has appeared on television in *Unbreakable Kimmy Schmidt* (Netflix), *Royal Pains* (USA), *Rules of Cool* (Fullscreen). She can be heard as a voiceover actor in these series and movies: *True Detective* (HBO), *The Righteous Gemstones* (HBO), *Logan Lucky*, *Gemini Man*, *Hillbilly Elegy*. And she can be seen in films such as

Pitching Tents (Hulu), *1 Message* (Dish Network), and *Love*, for which she also won an award for best actress at the 2018 NYTF.

She began her production company, AKA Studio Productions, in 2011, and their work has been seen in 150+ film festivals. *Mulligan* (2018 LA Film Festival, 1st place Flickers RIIFF), *Rules of Cool* (Fullscreen), *Capital Advice* (ITV Fest), *Ace* (Toronto Inside Out Fest), *Photo Op* (Winner SENE Film), *Blindsight* (LA Shorts), *Absent Mind* (Toronto International Shorts), and *Beauty Mark* (LA Film Festival, distributed by The Orchard).

She is also a proud teacher, children's theatrical director, and #BYOP creative consultant to hundreds of clients and students, including teen prodigy Elise Marra, music artist behind the Billboard Top 10 album, *Frankie! The Musical*.

Up Next is *Boy Hero*, a feature film inspired by the comic book trial of 1954 which she wrote, produced, and will star in.

In her spare time, you can find Ashley Kate with her loved ones usually somewhere not too far from her beloved neighborhood of Long Island City. She also loves to listen, read, or watch the latest true crime series, and to attend (and celebrate!) the works of her creative friends.

Ashley Kate is represented by A3 Artists Agency.

Contact Ashley Kate and sign up for her email list on her website, www.ashleykateadams.com.

To support Ashley Kate's creative journey and projects, find her on Instagram at:

@ashleykateadams

@byop_nyc

@akastudiosnyc

@boyheromovie

@frankiemusical